OWASP
For Secure Web Applications

Rajesh Dangi

July 2024, Bengaluru.

To my fellow developers...

"Writing a secure web application starts at the architecture phase. A vulnerability discovered in this phase can cost as much as 60 times less than a vulnerability found in production code."

Table of contents

Preface

The digital landscape is in a state of perpetual flux, making web application security an uncompromising priority. Our interconnected environment exposes us to a vast array of threats, ranging from sophisticated cyberattacks to seemingly trivial misconfigurations that can have cascading consequences. As developers, engineers, and security professionals, we have a professional obligation to not only comprehend these risks but also possess the expertise and tools to effectively mitigate them. Proactive security is no longer a luxury; it's a fundamental tenet of responsible software development.

This book serves as an insight for leveraging the Open Web Application Security Project (OWASP) framework to construct robust web applications. OWASP, a global non-profit organization at the forefront of software security advancement, provides a wealth of invaluable resources, methodologies, and best practices that empower us to fortify our digital creations against a constantly expanding threat landscape.

Also, within these pages, you'll embark on a rigorous exploration of the OWASP Top 10, a well-established compendium of the most critical web application security risks. Each vulnerability will be meticulously examined, providing profound insights into its nature, potential impact, and most importantly, proven strategies for prevention and detection. Through relatable examples and real-world scenarios, we'll delve into the intricacies of broken access controls, cryptographic flaws, injection attacks, insecure design principles, misconfigurations, and more. You'll gain the ability to not only identify these vulnerabilities but also implement robust countermeasures to safeguard your applications.

OWASP guidance is a strategic for integrating security into the very foundation of the software development lifecycle (SDLC). From threat modelling and secure coding practices to penetration testing and agile methodologies, we'll explore how to seamlessly weave OWASP principles into your development processes. You'll discover how to identify security risks early in the development process, ensuring that security is not a secondary consideration but a fundamental tenet from the very beginning. This shift towards a security-conscious development culture is essential for building applications that are not only functional but also inherently resistant to attacks. Furthermore, this book acts as a gateway to the extensive library of OWASP projects and resources available to the security community. Whether you seek industry-standard testing tools, concise reference guides, or in-depth guidance on building a secure SDLC, OWASP provides a wealth of resources to fuel your journey towards building more resilient and secure web applications.

As we embark on this collaborative endeavour, I encourage you to approach each chapter with an inquiring mind and a commitment to applying these principles in your own professional pursuits. By embracing the OWASP philosophy and adopting a proactive security posture, we can collectively forge a more secure and resilient digital future. Thank you for joining me on this exploration of OWASP for secure web applications and urge you to refer https://owasp.org/ for detailed documentation for deeper understanding of all concepts, projects and applications to take this journey forward. Together, let's champion the movement towards a safer online world, where innovation thrives alongside robust security measures.

Regs,

Rajesh Dangi, 2024

Bangalore, India

~ P.S. - As much precaution is taken while writing on simplification of technological jargons via analogical explanations and curated narratives, any lapses to be excused. The book is designed in a way to help read each section / topic independently and by any order based on the reader's interest. The narrative is shaped using publicly available online AI/LLM tools to shape up my linguistic barriers, thus, to be excused on the repetitive content references in the narrative and pardon third person perspectives thereof.

OWASP Introduction

The digital landscape is a churning sea of innovation, constantly transforming the way we connect, interact, and conduct business. However, amidst this progress lurks a shadow; the ever-present threat of cyberattacks. Web applications, the engines driving much of this digital activity, have become a prime target for malicious actors. A single security vulnerability, a chink in the armour, can have a devastating ripple effect, exposing sensitive data, disrupting critical operations, eroding user trust, and inflicting substantial financial damage.

In this ever-shifting landscape, the Open Web Application Security Project (OWASP - https://owasp.org/) emerges as a beacon of hope, illuminating a path towards secure development practices. OWASP isn't a singular product or service; it's a global, non-profit community dedicated to empowering individuals and organizations to build secure web applications. Imagine a vast treasure trove filled with free resources, methodologies, best practices, and even testing tools; that's the essence of OWASP. Its extensive library caters to a wide range of expertise, from seasoned developers to those just embarking on their development journey. OWASP equips you with the knowledge and tools to fortify your creations against the ever-present threats that plague the digital world.

The urgency of secure development practices cannot be overstated. In the bygone era, security might have been relegated to an afterthought, a layer hastily bolted onto an application after it was built. However, the digital landscape has morphed into a digital battlefield, with sophisticated attackers constantly probing for weaknesses. A data breach isn't just a technical hiccup; it can cripple your business, erode user trust which is a vital commodity in today's digital age and take years to rebuild. The financial repercussions can be equally devastating, with regulatory fines and lawsuits adding insult to injury. By embracing OWASP principles and integrating security into every phase of the development lifecycle, we can proactively address vulnerabilities before they morph into critical issues.

This shift towards "secure by design" is no longer a luxury; it's a fundamental tenet of responsible software development.

Key aspects of OWASP include...

- Documentation: OWASP produces a wide range of resources, including the OWASP Top Ten, a regularly updated list of the most critical security risks facing web applications. This list helps organizations prioritize their security efforts by highlighting common vulnerabilities and providing guidance on mitigation strategies.
- Tools and Projects: OWASP sponsors and supports numerous open-source projects and tools aimed at improving web application security. These projects cover various aspects of security testing, vulnerability scanning, code analysis, and security education.
- Community Engagement: OWASP fosters a vibrant community of security professionals and enthusiasts who collaborate through local chapters, conferences, meetups, and online forums. These interactions facilitate knowledge sharing, networking, and skill development within the field of web application security.
- Education and Training: OWASP promotes security awareness and education by offering training courses, workshops, and educational materials. These resources help developers and security practitioners enhance their understanding of web application security principles and best practices.
- Advocacy: OWASP advocates for improved security standards and practices across the industry. It engages with policymakers, standards organizations, and industry stakeholders to raise awareness of security issues and promote the adoption of secure development methodologies.

By working together and harnessing the collective wisdom of OWASP, we can forge a more secure digital future, one web application at a time. This collaborative approach, fostered by the resources and community provided by OWASP, is essential for building applications that are not only functional but also inherently resistant to attacks. This collaborative effort ensures that security is not an afterthought, but a foundational principle woven into the very DNA of the application, from conception to deployment.

Demystifying OWASP - Role in Web Application Security

Imagine a bustling marketplace overflowing with vendors hawking their wares. This marketplace represents the digital landscape, teeming with innovative web applications that cater to our every need. But amidst the dazzling displays and enticing functionalities lurks a hidden danger – vulnerabilities. These vulnerabilities are akin to cracks in the walls of a fortress, invisible to the untrained eye but ripe for exploitation by malicious actors.

Here's where OWASP steps in, acting as a trusted security consultant in this digital marketplace. It doesn't sell any specific product or service; instead, it offers a wealth of freely available resources – think guidebooks, checklists, and even tools to help developers, engineers, and security professionals build applications with robust security in mind.

Decoding the acronym – Open Web Application Security Project

- **Open**: Accessibility is paramount in the ethos of OWASP. By being open, OWASP ensures that its wealth of resources, knowledge, and expertise are freely available to anyone who seeks them. This openness fosters a collaborative and inclusive environment where individuals from diverse backgrounds and expertise levels can come together to share insights, best practices, and solutions. It's this open exchange of ideas that propels innovation and drives continuous improvement in the field of web application security.

- **Web Application**: In today's digital landscape, web applications serve as the backbone of much of our online activity. From e-commerce platforms to social media networks, these dynamic and interactive applications facilitate communication, commerce, and entertainment. However, they also represent a prime target for malicious actors seeking to exploit vulnerabilities for nefarious purposes. Recognizing the critical role that web applications play in our daily lives, OWASP directs its primary focus towards securing these vital components of the internet ecosystem.

- **Security Project**: Security is not merely an afterthought or an add-on feature; it's a project by itself. OWASP understands that safeguarding web applications requires a proactive and comprehensive approach that permeates every stage of the development lifecycle. As a security project, OWASP provides a robust framework, methodologies, and tools aimed at integrating security seamlessly into the fabric of software development. From threat modelling and secure coding practices to penetration testing and vulnerability management, OWASP equips developers and security professionals with the resources they need to build resilient and secure web applications from the ground up.

OWASP thus embodies the principles of openness, specialization, and proactivity in its mission to enhance the security of web applications worldwide. By decoding the OWASP acronym, we gain insight into the organization's core values and objectives, laying the foundation for a collaborative and secure digital future. (https://owasp.org/)

OWASP's Multifaceted Role

OWASP plays a multifaceted role in the realm of web application security, encompassing several key functions

Knowledge Dissemination

As a knowledge hub, OWASP offers a vast array of educational resources aimed at enhancing understanding and awareness of web application security concepts. Through articles, tutorials, cheat sheets, and other materials, OWASP equips individuals with the knowledge and skills needed to identify, mitigate, and prevent security risks effectively.

Standardization

OWASP serves as a champion for industry best practices and methodologies in web application security. By advocating for standardized approaches to security, OWASP promotes consistency and a common understanding of security practices within the development community. This standardization helps streamline security efforts, making it easier for developers and organizations to implement robust security measures across their projects.

Community Building

OWASP cultivates a dynamic and inclusive global community of developers, security professionals, and enthusiasts passionate about web application security. Through events, forums, and collaborative projects, OWASP provides a platform for individuals to connect, collaborate, and share insights and experiences. This vibrant community fosters a culture of collaboration and knowledge sharing, driving continuous improvement and innovation in web application security.

Empowerment

One of OWASP's primary objectives is to empower developers with the tools, resources, and knowledge they need to build secure web applications. By arming developers with comprehensive security guidance and best practices, OWASP enables them to take ownership of security within their projects. This empowerment fosters a proactive approach to security, where vulnerabilities are identified and addressed early in the development process, rather than as an afterthought. Ultimately, this proactive stance helps mitigate security risks and enhance the overall security posture of web applications.

OWASP's multifaceted role encompasses knowledge dissemination, standardization, community building, and empowerment, all working together to advance the field of web application security and create a safer digital environment for all users.

The Urgency of OWASP - Why Secure Development Matters Now

The digital landscape is no longer the Wild West of the early internet; the stakes are much higher. In today's interconnected world, web applications play a critical role in everything from online banking and e-commerce to managing healthcare records and critical infrastructure. A single security breach can have catastrophic consequences, leading to...

Data Breaches

The digital age has ushered in an era of unprecedented convenience and connectivity. However, amidst the undeniable benefits lurks a chilling threat the specter of data breaches. As the volume of sensitive information entrusted to the digital realm continues to proliferate, so too does the risk of its exposure. These breaches, often the result of sophisticated cyberattacks or human error, can have a devastating ripple effect, impacting individuals, organizations, and even entire industries.

The Human Cost of Data Breaches

The consequences of a data breach extend far beyond a mere inconvenience. The very information that fuels our online interactions – financial data, social security numbers, medical records, and even private communications becomes a weapon in the hands of malicious actors. Identity theft, a crime where stolen personal information is used to impersonate a victim, can wreak havoc on a person's financial standing and credit score. Imagine the sinking feeling of discovering unauthorized charges on your credit card or loans taken out in your name – the aftereffects of identity theft can be a long and arduous journey of financial recovery and emotional distress.

The emotional toll of a data breach can be equally significant. The sense of violation and a loss of privacy can be deeply unsettling. Individuals may become wary of online interactions, leading to a general distrust of the digital ecosystem.

How Data Breaches Cripple Organizations

For organizations, the repercussions of a data breach can be catastrophic. Financial losses can be substantial, encompassing not only the cost of notifying affected individuals and regulatory fines, but also the potential for lawsuits and reputational damage. Regaining the trust of customers and stakeholders can be a long and arduous process. In today's competitive landscape, a tarnished reputation can translate to lost business and a decline in customer loyalty.

The fallout from a data breach can extend beyond immediate financial losses. The organization's internal morale might plummet as employees grapple with the aftermath of the breach. Furthermore, a data breach can have a chilling effect on innovation, as organizations may become overly cautious and hesitant to embrace new technologies.

Protecting Our Digital Landscape - Collective Responsibility

The responsibility for safeguarding our digital landscape from data breaches extends beyond any single entity. Individuals must practice good online hygiene, using strong passwords, enabling two-factor authentication, and remaining vigilant for phishing attempts. Organizations must prioritize robust security measures, investing in secure infrastructure, implementing rigorous access controls, and fostering a culture of security awareness among employees.

Disrupted Operations

Web applications serve as the lifeblood of countless businesses and organizations, facilitating critical functions such as online transactions, communication, and data management. They are the engines that power our online interactions, handling everything from online banking and e-commerce transactions to communication platforms and data management tools. But what happens when these critical digital infrastructures come under attack? A successful cyberattack that compromises a web application can have a cascading effect, causing significant disruptions to operations and inflicting substantial financial and reputational losses. The impact of a web application disruption can be wide-ranging and far-reaching. Here's a closer look at the potential consequences…

- Downtime: A successful attack can render the web application completely inoperable. This can cause significant downtime, preventing users from accessing critical services. Imagine an online store being inaccessible during peak holiday shopping season, or a hospital's appointment scheduling system being unavailable during a surge in patient cases. The lost revenue and productivity can be immense. Customers who rely on these services may become frustrated and abandon their online transactions or interactions, leading to further losses.
- Lost Revenue: Beyond the immediate cost of downtime, businesses may incur additional financial losses. For instance, an e-commerce site experiencing a denial-of-service attack might lose out on potential sales during the crucial downtime. Financial institutions may face penalties for non-compliance with regulations if a security breach exposes sensitive customer data. In the healthcare industry, disruptions to appointment scheduling or insurance verification systems can lead to lost revenue opportunities and delayed care for patients.
- Damaged Reputation: A cyberattack can severely tarnish an organization's reputation. News of a security breach can erode user trust, leading to a decline in customer loyalty and a reluctance to engage with the organization's services. Rebuilding trust takes time and significant effort. Customers who have had negative experiences due to a web application disruption may be hesitant to use the service again, and may even share their

negative experiences with others, further damaging the organization's brand image.

Vulnerable Industries - The High Stakes of Disruption

Certain industries are particularly susceptible to the devastating consequences of web application disruptions. Here are some prime examples...

- Healthcare: Hospitals and clinics rely heavily on web applications for managing patient records, scheduling appointments, and facilitating communication with healthcare providers. An attack that disrupts these applications can delay critical medical care and even put lives at risk. Disruptions to online appointment scheduling systems can lead to frustrated patients and a backlog of appointments, further straining healthcare resources.
- Finance: The uninterrupted operation of web applications is paramount in the financial sector, where online banking, investment platforms, and payment processing systems are vital. A cyberattack that compromises these applications can disrupt financial transactions, cause significant financial losses for both the institution and its customers, and erode user trust in financial institutions. Customers who are unable to access their online accounts or make payments due to a web application disruption may lose confidence in the security of the institution's systems.
- E-commerce: For online retailers, web applications are the foundation of their business model. A cyberattack that disrupts their online store can lead to lost sales, damage customer confidence, and tarnish the brand reputation. Customers who encounter errors or are unable to complete their purchases due to a web application disruption may abandon their shopping carts and take their business elsewhere.

The potential consequences of web application disruptions highlight the importance of a proactive security posture. By prioritizing web application security and taking steps to mitigate these risks, organizations can safeguard their critical digital infrastructure, minimize downtime, and protect their bottom line. This not only ensures a smooth user experience but also fosters trust with their customers and stakeholders in the ever-evolving digital landscape.

Eroded User Trust

Trust is the lifeblood of online interactions. We entrust businesses and organizations with a wealth of sensitive information – financial data, health records, personal details – all underpinned by the expectation of security and privacy. However, a data breach or security incident can shatter this trust with a resounding blow, leaving a trail of frustration, anger, and a deep sense of vulnerability in its wake. The consequences of eroded user trust extend far beyond the immediate financial losses or operational disruptions an organization might face. Here's why a data breach can inflict such a heavy toll...

- Broken Promises, Broken Bonds: When a security incident occurs, it signifies a broken promise – a failure to safeguard the very information users entrusted to the organization's care. This betrayal of trust can lead to feelings of anger, resentment, and a sense of helplessness among users.
- Privacy Concerns Magnified: Data breaches expose users' most private information, potentially putting them at risk of identity theft, financial fraud, or even physical harm. This heightened sense of vulnerability can lead to a reluctance to engage with online services or share personal information altogether.
- Reputational Damage: News of a data breach can travel fast, tarnishing an organization's reputation. Social media can amplify negative experiences, leading to a public perception of the organization as careless or incompetent when it comes to data

security. Rebuilding a damaged reputation takes time, significant effort, and a demonstrably strong commitment to security.

Rebuilding Trust After a Breach

Regaining user trust after a data breach is an uphill battle. Here are some crucial steps organizations must take on the road to recovery...

- Transparency and Communication: Open and honest communication with affected users is paramount. This includes promptly informing them about the nature of the breach, the data that was compromised, and the steps being taken to address the vulnerability and prevent future incidents.
- Accountability and Action: Taking responsibility for the breach and demonstrating a commitment to improving security posture is essential. This might involve implementing stronger security measures, conducting thorough security audits, and even offering identity theft protection services to affected users.
- Earning Back Trust: Rebuilding trust is a long-term process. Organizations must demonstrate a sustained commitment to data security through their actions. This might involve obtaining industry-recognized security certifications, investing in security awareness training for employees, and fostering a culture of security within the organization.

The Importance of Proactive Security

The potential consequences of eroded user trust highlight the importance of a proactive approach to security. By prioritizing robust security measures, organizations can minimize the risk of data breaches and safeguard user trust – the cornerstone of a successful online presence. Remember, user trust is a fragile commodity; once broken, it takes time, dedication, and demonstrably improved security practices to win it back. Investing in security is not just about protecting data; it's about safeguarding the very foundation of your relationship with your users.

Regulatory Fines

The regulatory landscape surrounding data privacy and security has become increasingly stringent in response to growing cybersecurity threats. Data breaches can trigger significant fines and penalties from regulatory bodies, compounding the financial impact of a security incident. Organizations may also face legal repercussions and reputational damage, further amplifying the consequences of inadequate security measures.

India's digital landscape is experiencing a data deluge, and with it comes a heightened responsibility to safeguard user privacy. The government has responded with a robust legal framework to ensure data security, creating a multi-pronged attack on organizations with lax security practices. Here's why a data breach can trigger a domino effect of financial and reputational repercussions in India...

Beyond the Breach - A Web of Regulatory Fines

While the immediate costs of a data breach involve notifying users and recovery measures, the financial repercussions in India can be substantial. Unlike some other jurisdictions, India enforces data privacy through a combination of central and sectoral regulations, creating a layered web of potential fines...

- The Information Technology Act (IT Act), 2000 and its amendments: This act, along with its associated Information Technology (Reasonable Security Practices and Procedures and Sensitive Personal Data or Information) Rules, 2011, mandates reasonable security practices for organizations handling sensitive personal data. Non-compliance can lead to imprisonment of up to three years or a fine of up to ₹5 lakh (approximately $6,600 USD), or both.
- The Digital Personal Data Protection Act (DPDP Act, 2023): This recently enacted law establishes a more comprehensive data

security regime. The DPDP Act empowers the central government to impose tiered penalties based on the severity of the offense and the sensitivity of the data compromised. Fines can reach up to ₹250 crore (approximately $33 million USD) for contraventions.

- Sectoral Regulations: Certain sectors in India, such as healthcare and finance, have their own data privacy regulations that can impose additional fines for non-compliance in the event of a data breach. For example, the Reserve Bank of India (RBI) has its own data security guidelines for the banking sector.
- Government Directions: The Indian government also issues directions and advisories from time to time to strengthen data security practices. Following these guidelines demonstrates a proactive approach to data privacy, which can be viewed favourably by regulators and the public.

The potential for cumulative fines from multiple regulations can be financially crippling, especially for smaller organizations. Regulatory fines are just the first step in the domino effect triggered by a data breach in India. Here's how lax security can further amplify the consequences...

- Reputational Damage: News of a data breach and hefty regulatory fines can severely tarnish an organization's reputation. Being labelled as non-compliant with data privacy regulations can erode user trust and damage brand image. Social media can amplify the negative publicity, making it even more challenging to regain public trust.
- Legal Repercussions: Beyond regulatory fines, data breaches can also lead to legal battles in India. Affected users or even government agencies may file lawsuits against the organization for failing to protect their data. These lawsuits can be costly to defend, even if the organization ultimately prevails.

In today's digital age, user trust is a valuable commodity. Demonstrating a commitment to data security through compliance with all applicable laws and regulations showcases your organization's trustworthiness and fosters stronger relationships with customers and stakeholders in the Indian market. Regulatory compliance signifies that your organization takes data privacy seriously. This can be a significant competitive advantage, especially when dealing with partners and vendors who prioritize data security in the Indian landscape.

The financial and reputational costs associated with data breaches and regulatory non-compliance highlight the importance of prioritizing security. By implementing robust security measures that align with all applicable laws, regulations, and government directions in India, organizations can minimize the risk of data breaches, safeguard user trust, and establish themselves as credible players in the Indian digital landscape. Remember, data privacy is not just about compliance; it's about building trust, protecting user data, and fostering a secure and thriving digital ecosystem for everyone in India.

In such high-stakes environment, the imperative to prioritize web application security has never been clearer. Organizations must adopt a proactive approach to security, implementing robust measures to safeguard against cyber threats and mitigate the potential fallout of security incidents. The cost of a security breach can be staggering. Beyond the immediate financial losses, there's the intangible cost of reputational damage. Regaining the trust of users and customers can take years of diligent effort. The paradigm of security as an afterthought is no longer sustainable. Secure development practices are not a luxury; they are a fundamental requirement. By integrating security into every phase of the development lifecycle, from design to deployment, we can proactively identify and address vulnerabilities before they morph into critical issues.

This "security by design" approach is the cornerstone of OWASP's philosophy, and it's the key to building web applications that are not only functional but also inherently resistant to attacks. By embracing the principles championed by OWASP, we can collectively build a more secure digital future, one web application at a time.

Mastering the OWASP Top 10

The OWASP Top 10 isn't merely a numbered list; it's a powerful arsenal in your fight against critical web application security risks. This curated compendium exposes the ten most prevalent vulnerabilities that malicious actors leverage to compromise applications. By gaining a comprehensive understanding of these risks, you can significantly fortify your application's defenses and proactively thwart attacks.

The Top 10 - Empowering Developers with Knowledge

In-Depth Vulnerability Analysis

Each entry in the Top 10 meticulously dissects a specific vulnerability, providing clear explanations of its technical nature, the potential impact on your application's security posture, and most importantly, proven prevention and detection strategies. This empowers developers to not only identify these vulnerabilities but also implement robust countermeasures to safeguard the application throughout its lifecycle.

The OWASP Top 10 serves as a comprehensive guidebook, offering developers invaluable insights into the most prevalent and critical security risks facing web applications today. Through meticulous analysis, each vulnerability is thoroughly examined, shedding light on its underlying mechanisms and potential ramifications. Armed with this knowledge, developers gain a deeper understanding of the threats they face, allowing them to make informed decisions and implement effective security measures.

Moreover, the Top 10 goes beyond merely identifying vulnerabilities; it provides actionable guidance on prevention and detection strategies. By offering clear and practical recommendations, developers can proactively mitigate risks and fortify their applications against potential attacks. This proactive approach not only enhances the security posture of individual applications but also contributes to a more resilient digital ecosystem.

Prioritized Focus

The Top 10 functions as a risk stratification tool, highlighting the most prevalent and impactful vulnerabilities that should be addressed with the utmost urgency. By focusing your development security efforts on these high-risk areas, you can maximize the return on your investment in terms of security improvements.

In a world of finite resources and competing priorities, prioritization is key to effectively managing security risks. The Top 10 serves as a roadmap, guiding developers towards the vulnerabilities that pose the greatest threat to their applications. By identifying and prioritizing these high-risk areas, developers can allocate their resources more efficiently, ensuring that security efforts are directed where they are needed most.

Furthermore, the Top 10's prioritized focus enables developers to make informed decisions about risk mitigation strategies. By tackling the most critical vulnerabilities first, developers can achieve significant security improvements with limited resources. This targeted approach not only enhances the overall security posture of applications but also helps organizations make more strategic investments in security.

Standardized Security Language

The Top 10 fosters a common understanding of security risks across diverse development teams. This standardized language ensures that everyone involved in the development process, from programmers to security professionals, speaks the same language concerning security threats. This not only streamlines communication but also fosters a collaborative environment where security becomes a shared responsibility.

Effective communication is essential for successful collaboration, especially when it comes to security. The Top 10 serves as a common language that unites developers, security professionals, and other stakeholders, enabling them to effectively communicate about security risks and mitigation strategies. This shared understanding fosters collaboration and teamwork, breaking down silos and promoting a culture of security across the organization.

Moreover, the standardized language of the Top 10 facilitates knowledge sharing and education, empowering developers to become more security-conscious in their day-to-day work. By speaking a common language, developers can more easily access and understand security-related resources, enabling them to make informed decisions and take proactive measures to secure their applications.

Navigating the Ever-Evolving Threat Landscape

Armed with the knowledge gleaned from the OWASP Top 10, you'll be well-equipped to recognize and mitigate common web application vulnerabilities that have plagued the digital world for years. These vulnerabilities include, but are not limited to...

Broken Access Control

This vulnerability arises when an application's access control mechanisms are misconfigured or weak, allowing unauthorized users to access sensitive data or functionalities. Imagine a bank vault overflowing with valuables, but the security guard is asleep, and the front door is wide open. That's essentially what a Broken Access Control vulnerability represents in the digital world. This critical security flaw arises when an application's access control mechanisms are weak or misconfigured, allowing unauthorized users to waltz right in and access sensitive data or functionalities that they shouldn't have any business with. Here's a deeper dive into this vulnerability and its potential consequences...

The Many Faces of Broken Access Control

Broken Access Control can manifest in various ways, each posing a significant security risk...

- Missing or Weak Authentication: In some cases, applications might lack proper authentication mechanisms altogether, allowing anyone to access them freely. Alternatively, the authentication process might be weak, relying on easily guessable passwords or outdated security protocols. Think of a simple padlock on your vault; while it might deter casual passers by a determined attacker can easily break through.
- Improper Authorization: Even if an application requires users to log in, authorization controls might be poorly implemented. This

could allow users to access functionalities or data beyond their designated permissions. Imagine a bank teller who can not only process withdrawals but also manipulate account balances – a recipe for disaster.

- Privilege Escalation: Attackers might exploit vulnerabilities in the application to elevate their privileges from a standard user to an administrator. This would grant them complete control over the application, allowing them to steal data, modify settings, or even deploy malware. Imagine a bank robber who not only gets access to the vault but also gains control of the entire security system.

The Devastating Consequences of a Broken Gate

- Data Breaches: Unauthorized access to sensitive data is a major risk. This could include personal information like customer details, financial data, or intellectual property. A data breach can not only result in financial losses but also erode user trust and damage an organization's reputation.
- Disrupted Operations: Attackers might exploit access control flaws to disrupt critical functionalities within an application. This could lead to outages, service disruptions, and financial losses. Imagine an online store where attackers can manipulate inventory or disable the checkout process, causing significant financial losses.
- Malware Deployment: Gaining unauthorized access can be a stepping stone for deploying malware within an application. This malware could then spread to other systems on the network, causing further damage. Imagine a bank robber who not only steals money but also plants a device to disable the alarm system for future heists.

Injection Attacks

Imagine a baker carefully crafting a delicious cake, only to have a mischievous prankster sneak in some unwanted ingredients. That's the essence of an Injection Attack in the digital world. Attackers exploit vulnerabilities in how applications handle user input, essentially injecting malicious code disguised as legitimate data. This injected code then gets executed by the application itself, potentially causing severe damage.

The Arsenal of the Injection Attacker

- SQL Injection (SQLi): This notorious attack targets applications that rely on databases. Attackers inject malicious SQL code into user inputs like search bars or login forms. Once executed by the database, this code can steal sensitive data, modify databases, or even grant the attacker unauthorized access. Imagine the baker's prankster slipping in a recipe that steals all the delicious ingredients from the bakery's inventory!
- Cross-Site Scripting (XSS): This attack injects malicious scripts, often JavaScript, into user inputs displayed on web pages. When another user views the page, the script gets executed in their browser, potentially stealing their session cookies, redirecting them to phishing sites, or even defacing the website itself. Think of the prankster replacing the cake's delicious filling with something unpleasant, tricking unsuspecting customers!

The Devastating Consequences of Injected Code

- Data Breaches: Attackers can steal sensitive information like customer records, financial data, or intellectual property by manipulating database queries or stealing session cookies. This can lead to financial losses, identity theft, and reputational damage.
- System Compromise: In some cases, attackers can gain complete control of a system or server through successful injection attacks. This can be used to deploy malware, disrupt operations, or launch further attacks on other systems. Imagine the prankster taking

over the entire bakery's operations, causing chaos and potential food poisoning!

- Website Defacement: Attackers might use XSS to deface websites with malicious content or propaganda. This can damage an organization's reputation and erode user trust. Imagine the prankster replacing the bakery' signage with something offensive, turning away customers.

Insecure Design

Flawed design principles can create inherent vulnerabilities within an application. The Top 10 emphasizes the importance of secure design practices from the get-go, ensuring that security considerations are woven into the very fabric of the application from the initial design phase.

Imagine constructing a magnificent castle, only to realize the foundation is made of sand. That's the inherent danger of Insecure Design in the digital world. While features and functionalities are important, a secure application starts with a solid foundation; a design that prioritizes security from the very beginning. The OWASP Top 10 emphasizes this critical principle: security shouldn't be an afterthought; it should be woven into the fabric of the application from the initial design phase.

The Pitfalls of Flawed Design

Insecure design practices can create a breeding ground for vulnerabilities, leaving your application susceptible to a wide range of attacks...

- Weak Authentication: Flawed design choices might lead to weak authentication mechanisms, such as relying solely on passwords or having easily guessable default credentials. This is like building your castle with a flimsy wooden door — easily breached by even the most casual intruder.
- Inadequate Data Encryption: Sensitive data like user credentials or financial information might be stored in plain text or with weak

encryption algorithms. Imagine leaving your castle's treasure vault wide open, with no locks or guards to protect its riches.

- Improper Handling of Sensitive Information: The application might not have adequate controls in place to handle sensitive data securely. This could involve unnecessary data collection, insecure transmission methods, or inadequate disposal procedures. Think of leaving treasure maps scattered around the castle, making it easy for thieves to find your valuables.

The Domino Effect of Insecure Design

- Data Breaches: Inadequate security measures leave sensitive data vulnerable to breaches, exposing users to identity theft and financial losses. This can lead to a loss of trust and damage the organization's reputation. Imagine your castle being breached, leading to the loss of your most prized possessions.
- System Compromise: Security vulnerabilities can be exploited by attackers to gain unauthorized access to systems or networks. This can disrupt operations, deploy malware, or launch further attacks. Think of attackers taking over your entire castle, using it as a base for further conquests.
- Compliance Issues: Failure to adhere to data security regulations can result in hefty fines and legal repercussions. Imagine your castle being deemed structurally unsound and facing sanctions from the authorities.

Out-of-Date Components

Using outdated and unpatched software libraries within your application creates exploitable entry points for attackers. The Top 10 highlights the importance of implementing robust patch management strategies to keep all software components up-to-date and secure.

Imagine a magnificent knight clad in gleaming armour, ready to defend the realm. But upon closer inspection, you discover a chink in the armour, a rusty, outdated piece that offers little protection. This vulnerability represents the risk of Outdated Components in the digital world. While your application might boast impressive features, relying on outdated and unpatched software libraries is like having a weakness waiting to be exploited. The OWASP Top 10 emphasizes the importance of robust patch management, a proactive approach to keeping all software components within your application up-to-date and secure.

Why Outdated Components are a Threat.

Third-party libraries, frameworks, and dependencies are the building blocks of many modern applications. While these components offer convenience and functionality, they can also introduce security risks...

- Exploited Vulnerabilities: Security researchers constantly discover vulnerabilities in software. Attackers are quick to exploit these known vulnerabilities, targeting applications that haven't been patched. This is like the enemy discovering a weakness in the knight's outdated armour and focusing their attack there.
- Expanded Attack Surface: Each outdated component adds to the overall attack surface of your application. The more components you have, the more potential entry points for attackers to exploit. Imagine the knight having multiple outdated pieces of armour, creating more vulnerable areas for attack.
- Supply Chain Attacks: A vulnerability in a single, widely used component can create a ripple effect, impacting numerous applications that rely on it. This is like a single, undetected weakness in the knight's armour supplier putting an entire army at risk.

The consequences of failing to address outdated components can be severe...

- Data Breaches: Attackers can exploit vulnerabilities in outdated components to gain unauthorized access to sensitive user data. This can lead to financial losses, identity theft, and reputational damage. Imagine the enemy breaching the knight's outdated armour, stealing valuable intel or harming the kingdom.
- System Compromise: In some cases, attackers can gain complete control of a system by exploiting vulnerabilities in outdated components. This can be used to deploy malware, disrupt operations, or launch further attacks. Think of the enemy using the breached armour to take over the knight and use them to infiltrate the castle.
- Compliance Issues: Failure to maintain up-to-date software can violate data security regulations, resulting in hefty fines and legal repercussions. Imagine the knight facing sanctions for using outdated and unsafe equipment.

By understanding these prevalent threats and incorporating secure coding practices throughout the development lifecycle, you can significantly reduce the attack surface of your web application.

Integrating the OWASP Top 10 into Your Development Process

The true power of the OWASP Top 10 lies in its proactive application throughout the development process. Here are some key takeaways to leverage the Top 10 for maximum impact...

Threat Modelling

During the design phase, leverage the OWASP Top 10 as a threat modelling framework to proactively identify potential security risks associated with your application's architecture and functionalities.

The Indian digital landscape is experiencing a surge in user activity, necessitating a heightened focus on data security. For application developers, ensuring the confidentiality, integrity, and availability of user data is paramount. A critical component of this security posture is threat modelling, a systematic approach to identifying and mitigating potential security risks early in the development lifecycle.

The OWASP Top 10 as a Threat Modelling Framework

The Open Web Application Security Project (OWASP) Top 10 serves as an invaluable resource for developers in India. This industry-standard list categorizes the ten most critical web application security risks. By leveraging the OWASP Top 10 as a threat modelling framework, developers can proactively identify vulnerabilities associated with their application's architecture and functionalities. This enables them to make informed decisions about security measures from the very beginning of the design phase.

Benefits of Proactive Threat Modelling

- Early Threat Identification: By adopting a security-first mindset and anticipating potential attacks, developers can address vulnerabilities before they become exploitable weaknesses. This proactive approach is akin to conducting a thorough risk assessment for a building project, identifying potential structural flaws before construction commences.

- Security by Design: Threat modelling allows developers to integrate security measures into the foundational fabric of the application. This is analogous to incorporating firewalls and access control systems into the blueprints of a building, rather than retrofitting them later.

- Reduced Development Costs: Addressing security vulnerabilities early in the development cycle is significantly more cost-effective than fixing them after deployment. Imagine identifying and rectifying a potential fire hazard during the planning stage, saving time and resources compared to rebuilding a burnt section later.

- Enhanced Application Security: By proactively mitigating security risks, developers can create more secure and resilient applications. This translates to a lower risk of data breaches, system compromise, and reputational damage, fostering trust with users and potentially reducing the financial impact of regulatory non-compliance in India's evolving legal landscape.

The Threat Modelling Process

Threat modelling is a structured process that can be tailored to the specific needs of an application. Here's a general outline:

- Define the Scope: Clearly identify the application's functionalities, data assets, and target audience. This initial step is akin to understanding the size, purpose, and occupants of a building project.

- Identify Threats: Using the OWASP Top 10 as a guide, developers brainstorm potential security threats based on the application's design. This involves thinking like an attacker and identifying vulnerabilities in areas such as Broken Access Control or Injection Attacks.

- Analyze Risks: Each identified threat is evaluated based on its likelihood of occurrence and potential impact on the application and its users. This risk analysis is like prioritizing potential hazards based on the building's structure and location (e.g., a fire in a high-rise office building poses a greater risk than one in a single-story bungalow).

- Mitigate Risks: Develop and implement appropriate security controls to address the identified threats. This involves choosing the most effective countermeasures, analogous to selecting appropriate security measures for the building project, such as fire alarms, sprinkler systems, or security guards.

- Document and Maintain: The threat modelling process, identified risks, and implemented controls are documented for future reference. This ensures a clear record is maintained, similar to keeping detailed blueprints and safety protocols for a building.

- Continuous Improvement: Threat modelling is an iterative process that should be revisited throughout the development lifecycle. As the application evolves, so too should the threat model to ensure continued security. This ongoing process is akin to conducting regular building inspections and maintenance to identify and address any emerging safety concerns.

Secure Coding Practices

India's digital boom necessitates robust security measures to safeguard user data and applications. As the guardians of this digital domain, developers play a critical role in building secure applications. Secure coding practices are the building blocks of this digital fortress, ensuring applications are inherently resistant to common attacks.

The OWASP Top 10 - A Developer's Security Roadmap

The Open Web Application Security Project (OWASP) Top 10 serves as a vital resource for developers in India. This industry-standard list categorizes the ten most critical web application security risks. By adhering to secure coding principles aligned with the OWASP Top 10, developers can write code that is less susceptible to these vulnerabilities.

The Arsenal of a Secure Coder

- Input Validation: Rigorously validating all user inputs is a fundamental principle. This involves ensuring inputs conform to expected formats and don't contain malicious code. Imagine a vigilant guard at the gates of your digital fortress, carefully checking all incoming data for hidden weapons.
- Data Sanitization: Even validated data can harbour hidden threats. Sanitization practices remove any potentially harmful characters or code before processing them. Think of the guard carefully inspecting and removing any concealed weapons from seemingly harmless packages.
- Secure Coding Techniques: A vast array of secure coding techniques exist, each addressing specific vulnerabilities. This might involve using parameterized queries to prevent SQL injection or implementing proper session management to thwart unauthorized access. Imagine the guard being trained in various security protocols to counter different attack methods.
- Compliance with Regulations: Secure coding practices are essential for adhering to data privacy regulations in India, such as the DPDP Act. This helps organizations avoid hefty fines and legal repercussions.

Security Testing

Regularly conduct security testing throughout the development lifecycle using industry-standard tools and methodologies India's burgeoning digital landscape thrives on user trust. To maintain this trust, applications must be secure fortresses, constantly vigilant against potential attacks. Security testing plays a critical role in identifying and addressing vulnerabilities before they can be exploited.

The OWASP Top 10 - A Guide for Prioritized Testing

The Open Web Application Security Project (OWASP) Top 10 serves as a valuable resource for security testing in India. This list categorizes the ten most critical web application security risks. By incorporating the OWASP Top 10 into your testing strategy, you can prioritize testing efforts to ensure the most critical vulnerabilities are addressed first. Imagine having a prioritized list of areas to inspect within your digital fortress, focusing on the most critical weaknesses first.

The Security Testing Arsenal

- Penetration Testing: Simulating real-world attack scenarios is a powerful way to uncover vulnerabilities. Penetration testers act like ethical hackers, probing for weaknesses in your application's defenses. This is like conducting a mock siege on your digital fortress, identifying any potential breaches.
- Static Application Security Testing (SAST): Automated tools can analyze your codebase to identify potential vulnerabilities and coding practices that could lead to security issues. Imagine using advanced scanners to identify structural weaknesses within the walls of your fortress.
- Dynamic Application Security Testing (DAST): These tools simulate real-world attacks by crawling your application and identifying vulnerabilities that might be exploited by attackers. This is like having automated guards constantly patrolling the perimeter of your fortress, searching for any suspicious activity.

Staying Updated

The digital threat landscape is constantly evolving, with new attack techniques emerging all the time. The digital world is a battlefield in constant flux. New technologies and functionalities emerge at a rapid pace, but so do threats and attack vectors. In this dynamic landscape, developers in India play a critical role in safeguarding user data and applications. Staying updated with the latest security trends and threats is paramount to maintaining a strong defense.

The Evolving Threat Landscape

Cybercriminals are constantly innovating, devising new techniques to exploit vulnerabilities and breach security measures. Just like medieval armies developed new siege weapons, attackers develop sophisticated tools and tactics to target digital fortresses.

The OWASP Top 10: A Dynamic Roadmap

The Open Web Application Security Project (OWASP) Top 10 serves as an invaluable resource for developers in India. This list, however, is not static. OWASP recognizes the evolving threat landscape and regularly reviews and updates the Top 10 to reflect the most critical security risks. This ensures developers have access to the most current information to guide their security efforts. Imagine having a constantly updated blueprint of the enemy's siege tactics, allowing you to adapt your defenses accordingly.

The Benefits of Staying Updated

- Proactive Security: By being aware of the latest vulnerabilities and attack techniques, developers can take proactive steps to mitigate these risks before they can be exploited. This allows you to stay ahead of the curve, anticipating potential attacks and strengthening your digital defenses.

- Reduced Vulnerability Risk: New vulnerabilities are constantly discovered. Staying updated with the OWASP Top 10 ensures you are aware of the most pressing threats and can prioritize your security efforts to address them. This helps to minimize the attack surface of your application, making it a less attractive target.
- Enhanced Application Security: By continuously adapting your security practices to address the latest threats, you can significantly improve the overall security posture of your application. This translates to a lower risk of data breaches and a more trustworthy digital environment for Indian users.

By following these steps and integrating the OWASP Top 10 into your development process, you can significantly reduce the risk of security breaches and build web applications that are inherently secure and resilient against evolving threats. Remember, security is not a one-time fix; it's an ongoing process. The OWASP Top 10 serves as your roadmap on this continuous security journey, empowering you to build trust with your users and safeguard your valuable data.

Deep Dives into Top 10 Vulnerabilities

The Open Web Application Security Project (OWASP) Top 10 stands as an essential resource for organizations and developers invested in the security of web applications. This data-driven and community-backed list, meticulously compiled by a renowned security organization, offers a comprehensive guide to the most critical security risks plaguing web applications today.

The power of the OWASP Top 10 lies in its dynamic approach. By leveraging real-world data on security incidents and incorporating expert feedback, the list provides a continuously evolving perspective on the ever-shifting landscape of cyber threats. This focus on prevalent vulnerabilities empowers developers and organizations to take a proactive stance against common security pitfalls. The list prioritizes these vulnerabilities based on their severity and pervasiveness, allowing organizations to strategically allocate their security resources and focus on areas that pose the greatest risk.

Beyond a mere list of vulnerabilities, the OWASP Top 10 functions as a roadmap for secure development throughout the entire application lifecycle. By addressing the vulnerabilities outlined in the list, developers and security professionals can establish robust security measures as an intrinsic part of the development process. This comprehensive approach strengthens an organization's overall security posture, significantly reducing their susceptibility to cyberattacks.

The benefits of a strong security posture extend far beyond technical considerations. It fosters trust with users. By demonstrating a commitment to protecting data and safeguarding applications, organizations can cultivate stronger relationships with their user base. In today's digital age, where security breaches can be catastrophic, proactive security measures also serve to protect an organization's reputation. The OWASP Top 10 empowers organizations to take control of their security posture, minimizing the risk of breaches and safeguarding their hard-earned reputation.

Ultimately, the true value of the OWASP Top 10 lies in its ability to protect critical assets. Web applications often handle sensitive data and resources, making them prime targets for attackers. The OWASP Top 10 empowers organizations to take decisive steps to secure these critical assets from exploitation and compromise. By understanding and addressing the most critical vulnerabilities, developers, security professionals, and organizations can work together to create a safer digital environment for everyone. The OWASP Top 10 isn't just a list; it's a call to action for a more secure web, let us explore each one in the subsequent sections...

A01: Breaching the Walls - Broken Access Control

Broken Access Control, often likened to poorly guarded gates in a magnificent castle, represents a critical vulnerability where web applications fail to adequately restrict access to authorized users and functionalities. This vulnerability manifests in various forms, including insecure default configurations, missing authorization checks, and flaws in session management. Insecure default configurations may ship with pre-configured accounts featuring weak passwords or unnecessary privileges, leaving the application vulnerable to exploitation. Similarly, missing authorization checks fail to verify user permissions, potentially granting unauthorized access to sensitive data or functionalities. Additionally, session management flaws, such as session hijacking vulnerabilities, can be exploited by attackers to gain illicit access.

The consequences of Broken Access Control can be dire and far-reaching. Data breaches are a significant risk, as attackers exploit access control weaknesses to gain unauthorized access to sensitive user data, including financial information and personal details. Moreover, system compromise becomes a possibility, with attackers potentially seizing complete control of the system, deploying malware, or launching further attacks. Furthermore, compliance issues may arise, as failure to implement proper access controls can result in violations of data privacy regulations, leading to substantial fines and legal ramifications.

To mitigate the risks posed by Broken Access Control, several prevention and detection methods can be employed. The principle of least privilege is crucial, ensuring that users are granted only the minimum level of access necessary for their tasks, thus limiting potential damage from unauthorized access. Implementing multi-factor authentication (MFA), which incorporates additional authentication factors beyond passwords, strengthens access controls and enhances security. Regular access reviews should also be conducted to reassess user access privileges periodically and ensure they remain appropriate. Additionally, security monitoring, including the monitoring of access logs, enables the detection of suspicious activity and potential breaches, facilitating timely response and mitigation efforts.

The Impact of Broken Access Control

The consequences of broken access control can be severe:

- Data Breaches: Broken Access Control represents a critical vulnerability that can lead to severe data breaches. Attackers exploit these vulnerabilities to gain unauthorized access to sensitive user data, ranging from financial records to personal information. Such breaches not only result in financial losses for organizations but also cause significant reputational damage. Furthermore, they raise profound concerns regarding privacy, eroding user trust and confidence in the organization's ability to safeguard their data. To mitigate this risk, organizations must prioritize the implementation of robust access control measures, including stringent authentication mechanisms and granular authorization controls, to prevent unauthorized access and protect sensitive data from exploitation.
- System Compromise: Beyond data breaches, Broken Access Control can potentially compromise the entire system hosting the web application. Attackers leverage access control vulnerabilities to gain unauthorized access to administrative functionalities or system-level privileges. With such access, attackers can manipulate system configurations, deploy malicious software, or launch further attacks, undermining the integrity and security of the organization's infrastructure. To mitigate this risk, organizations must adopt a comprehensive security approach, including regular security assessments, continuous monitoring, and timely patch management. By proactively identifying and addressing access control vulnerabilities, organizations can strengthen their defenses and minimize the risk of system compromise.

- Compliance Issues: Inadequate access controls also raise compliance concerns, particularly regarding data privacy regulations and standards. Organizations are obligated to comply with regulations mandating the implementation of proper access controls to protect sensitive data from unauthorized access. Failure to meet these regulatory requirements can result in severe consequences, including substantial fines, legal liabilities, and damage to the organization's reputation. Therefore, organizations must ensure strict adherence to relevant regulatory frameworks by implementing robust access control mechanisms, conducting regular audits, and maintaining comprehensive documentation of access control policies and procedures. By demonstrating compliance with regulatory standards, organizations can enhance trust among stakeholders and mitigate the risk of legal and financial penalties associated with non-compliance.

Building a Robust Defense

A layered approach is crucial to fortify your defenses against BAC. Here's an arsenal of tools and technologies that can significantly strengthen your security posture...

- Centralized Control with Access Control Management Systems (ACMS): Imagine a central command center for access control. ACMS provide a unified platform to manage user permissions across your entire IT infrastructure. This streamlines access control policy enforcement, simplifies role-based access control (RBAC) assignment, and enables monitoring of user access activities. An ACMS allows you to implement the principle of least privilege (granting only the minimum access required) consistently across the organization, reducing the attack surface and potential damage from a compromised account.
- Identity and Access Management (IAM) Solutions: Think of IAM as a comprehensive security butler for your digital identities. IAM

solutions go beyond access control, encompassing the entire user identity lifecycle, from creation and management to authentication and access control. They allow for strong authentication mechanisms, like multi-factor authentication (MFA), and enforce fine-grained access controls based on user roles and attributes. IAM solutions can ensure that only authorized users have access to specific resources, and that their access is constantly monitored and reviewed.

- Privileged Access Management (PAM) Solutions: Privileged accounts are the crown jewels of your IT kingdom, and PAM solutions act as the royal guards. These solutions focus on securing privileged accounts and access to critical systems. PAM helps prevent unauthorized access, enforces the principle of least privilege, and monitors privileged activity to detect and respond to potential security incidents. By securing privileged accounts, PAM solutions significantly reduce the risk of attackers gaining access to the most sensitive systems and data within your organization.

- Multi-Factor Authentication (MFA) Solutions: Imagine adding a fingerprint scan or a one-time passcode to your password – that's the essence of MFA. MFA solutions add extra layers of security beyond passwords, requiring users to provide additional authentication factors. This significantly reduces the risk of unauthorized access even if a password is compromised. MFA makes it much more difficult for attackers to exploit stolen passwords or weak credentials to gain access to user accounts.

Enhancing Detection and Response

Early detection and response are vital for mitigating the impact of BAC vulnerabilities. Here are some tools and practices to consider...

- Security Information and Event Management (SIEM) Platforms: Think of SIEM platforms as security detectives, constantly analyzing clues. They aggregate and correlate security event data from various sources, including access logs and network traffic. This allows for real-time monitoring of access attempts, detection of suspicious behaviour, and prompt response to security incidents. SIEM platforms can identify unusual access patterns or attempted breaches from unauthorized locations, enabling security teams to investigate and respond swiftly.

- Web Application Firewalls (WAFs): WAFs act as gatekeepers for your web applications, inspecting and filtering incoming HTTP traffic. They can detect and block malicious requests, including those that attempt to bypass access controls. WAFs provide an additional layer of defense against common attack vectors used to exploit BAC vulnerabilities in web applications.

- Vulnerability Scanning and Penetration Testing Tools: Think of these as security audits for your systems. Vulnerability scanning tools and penetration testing tools proactively identify and assess BAC vulnerabilities in web applications and IT systems. This allows you to prioritize remediation efforts, address weaknesses before they can be exploited, and validate the effectiveness of your access control measures. Regular vulnerability scans and penetration tests help ensure that your defenses are up-to-date and can identify new or emerging BAC vulnerabilities that need to be addressed.

Comprehending Broken Access Control

Broken Access Control can be likened to a scenario within a fortified castle, where the gates, meant to serve as the primary line of defense, are inadequately guarded. In this analogy, individuals of any standing can freely enter through the gates, thereby gaining access to the castle's most sensitive areas. This metaphor encapsulates the essence of Broken Access Control in web applications, where the mechanisms designed to regulate and restrict user access to authorized functionalities and data are deficient or ineffective.

Like the vulnerability posed by unguarded castle gates, Broken Access Control in web applications occurs when these systems lack the necessary measures to differentiate between legitimate users with appropriate access rights and unauthorized individuals attempting to gain entry. This failure to enforce proper access controls compromises the security posture of web applications, exposing sensitive data and functionalities to potential exploitation and unauthorized access.

Broken Access - Reasons and Fixes

Broken Access Control (BAC) lurks as a menacing threat in the shadows of web applications. It essentially means the mechanisms that control who can access what within an application are flawed, creating vulnerabilities that malicious actors can exploit to wreak havoc. Let's delve deeper into some common ways BAC manifests and explore remediation strategies to fortify your application's defenses.

Insecure Default Configurations

Imagine a new house with all the doors unlocked and spare keys lying around. This is akin to insecure default configurations. Many web applications come pre-configured with built-in accounts that often have weak passwords or excessive privileges. If these defaults remain unchanged, they become gaping holes in your security posture, inviting attackers in.

Remediation

- Change default credentials immediately: Don't wait for a security breach to happen! Update default usernames and passwords for all built-in accounts upon initial setup. Enforce strong password policies that mandate complexity requirements (uppercase, lowercase, numbers, symbols) and regular password changes to make life difficult for attackers.

- Principle of Least Privilege: This principle is your mantra. Grant accounts only the minimum privileges required to perform their designated tasks. There's no need for everyone to have "admin" access! Implement role-based access control (RBAC) to assign permissions based on user roles and responsibilities.
- Disable unused accounts: If a default account is not required, disable it to eliminate potential attack vectors. Why keep the spare key lying around if nobody needs it?

Missing Authorization Checks

Think of a bouncer at a club who lets anyone walk in without checking their ID. This reflects missing authorization checks. When an application doesn't properly verify user permissions before processing requests, it might unintentionally grant access to unauthorized users. This can happen due to coding errors or inadequate validation mechanisms. Attackers can exploit these loopholes to manipulate the application, potentially accessing sensitive data or functionalities they shouldn't have permission for.

Remediation

- Implement robust authorization checks: Rigorously validate user permissions before granting access to any resources or functionalities. Ensure the application code enforces these checks consistently throughout the application. Don't let anyone sneak past the digital bouncer without proper authorization!
- Least Privilege Principle Revisited: This principle applies not just to accounts but also to specific actions within the application. Users should only have access to the data and functionalities they need to perform their jobs. For instance, an editor shouldn't be able to delete published articles.
- Regular code reviews: Conduct code reviews on a regular basis to identify and rectify any authorization check vulnerabilities that

might be introduced through errors or omissions. Proactive code review is like having a security guard who regularly patrols your digital walls to identify weaknesses.

Session Management Flaws

Imagine someone stealing your car keys and using them to drive off with your car. Session management flaws are similar. These vulnerabilities, such as session hijacking or fixation, allow attackers to steal or manipulate session tokens (like digital car keys) used to maintain user logins. With these stolen tokens, attackers can impersonate legitimate users and gain unauthorized access to their accounts. This can lead to a significant security breach, compromising sensitive data and putting user accounts at risk.

Remediation

- Secure session tokens: Don't just use any key for your car (or your web application)! Use secure session tokens that are difficult to forge or hijack. Implement techniques like HTTPS to encrypt communication between the user's browser and the application, preventing attackers from intercepting tokens in transit.
- Session timeouts: Automatically log out users after a period of inactivity. This minimizes the window of opportunity for attackers to exploit stolen tokens. Imagine your car automatically locking itself after a certain amount of time to deter theft.
- Consider stateless sessions: For specific use cases, explore stateless session architectures that don't rely on long-lived session tokens. Stateless sessions are like using a one-time passcode instead of a reusable car key, reducing the risk of session hijacking.

By understanding these common Broken Access Control vulnerabilities and implementing these best practices, developers and security professionals can significantly improve the security posture of their web applications. Remember, a secure application is built on a foundation of strong access control mechanisms. By ensuring only authorized users have access to the information and functionalities they need, you can create a more secure and trustworthy digital environment for everyone. This will not only safeguard your application from malicious actors but also foster trust with your users, who can be confident that their data is protected.

Prevention and Detection - Continuous Vigilance is Key

Remember, security is an ongoing process. Selecting and implementing the right tools depends on your organization's specific needs, compliance requirements, and budget. Don't forget the importance of regular assessments and monitoring of your defenses need constant vigilance to stay effective against ever-evolving threats. By employing a multi-layered approach that combines these tools and best practices, organizations can significantly reduce the risks associated with Broken Access Control and create a more secure digital environment. Here are some additional points to consider...

- Principle of Least Privilege: Adhering to the Principle of Least Privilege involves granting users only the minimum level of access necessary to perform their tasks effectively. By limiting access to only what is required, organizations reduce the potential impact of unauthorized access and minimize the risk of data breaches or system compromise. Implementing this principle ensures that users have access only to the resources and functionalities essential for their roles, mitigating the risk of exploitation by malicious actors seeking to escalate their privileges within the system.
- Multi-Factor Authentication (MFA): Multi-Factor Authentication enhances access control by requiring users to provide additional authentication factors beyond passwords before gaining access to the system. This additional layer of security significantly reduces the risk of unauthorized access, even if passwords are compromised. By incorporating authentication factors such as

security tokens, biometric identifiers, or one-time passcodes, organizations can strengthen authentication mechanisms and thwart unauthorized access attempts, thus bolstering the overall security posture of the system.

- Regular Access Reviews: Conducting regular access reviews is essential for ensuring that user access privileges remain appropriate and aligned with business requirements. By periodically reviewing user access rights and permissions, organizations can identify and mitigate potential access control issues, such as orphaned accounts, excessive permissions, or unauthorized access attempts. These reviews help maintain the integrity of access controls, prevent unauthorized access, and ensure compliance with security policies and regulatory requirements.

- Security Monitoring: Continuous security monitoring involves monitoring access logs and system activities to detect suspicious behaviour and potential security breaches in real-time. By analyzing access logs and monitoring user activities, organizations can identify anomalies, unauthorized access attempts, or suspicious patterns indicative of malicious activity. Early detection of security incidents enables organizations to respond promptly, mitigate risks, and prevent further compromise of sensitive data or systems. Implementing robust security monitoring solutions, such as intrusion detection systems (IDS) or security information and event management (SIEM) platforms, enhances the organization's ability to detect and respond to security threats effectively.

By adopting a comprehensive approach that combines prevention, detection, response, and ongoing vigilance, organizations can effectively mitigate the risks associated with Broken Access Control and safeguard their valuable data and systems from unauthorized access and exploitation.

A02: Cryptographic Failures

Demystifying Cryptography

Cryptography is the art of securing communication by scrambling data into an unreadable format and then decrypting it on the receiving end. Think of it as a secret code used to safeguard valuable messages.

At its core, cryptography involves transforming plaintext data into an unreadable format, known as ciphertext, using cryptographic algorithms and keys. This process, often referred to as encryption, obscures the original content of the message, rendering it incomprehensible to unauthorized individuals or adversaries who may intercept it during transmission. The encrypted message is then securely transmitted across communication channels to the intended recipient.

Upon reaching the recipient, the encrypted message undergoes decryption, a process that reverses the encryption and transforms the ciphertext back into its original plaintext form. Decryption requires the use of the appropriate cryptographic keys, which are known only to the authorized parties involved in the communication. By possessing the necessary decryption key, the recipient can effectively decipher the encrypted message and retrieve its original content, ensuring confidentiality and integrity throughout the communication process.

Analogous to a secret code, cryptography functions as a sophisticated method of encoding information, akin to writing a message in a language known only to the sender and recipient. This encrypted communication provides a secure means of transmitting sensitive or confidential data across networks, protecting it from eavesdroppers, hackers, and other malicious entities. By leveraging cryptographic techniques, organizations can safeguard valuable messages, financial transactions, personal information, and other critical data against unauthorized access, interception, and tampering, thereby preserving the confidentiality and privacy of sensitive information in an increasingly interconnected and digital world.

A Multi-Layered Approach to Secure Cryptography

While the core best practices for mitigating cryptographic failures have been outlined, a truly robust defense requires a multi-layered approach. Here's a deeper dive into each element...

Encryption Algorithm Selection and Updates

- Understanding Algorithm Suitability: Different algorithms are suited for various purposes. Symmetric algorithms like AES are ideal for bulk encryption, while asymmetric algorithms like RSA excel in digital signatures and key exchange. Choosing the right algorithm for the task ensures optimal security and performance.
- Staying Ahead of the Curve: Cryptography is an evolving field. What's considered secure today might become vulnerable tomorrow due to advancements in computing power or cryptanalysis techniques. Regularly consult with security professionals and industry resources to stay informed about the latest algorithm recommendations from organizations like NIST (National Institute of Standards and Technology).
- Future-Proofing with Key Length: When selecting algorithms, consider key length. Longer key lengths offer exponentially stronger encryption. While current computing power might not be able to crack a specific algorithm with a 2048-bit key, future advancements could make it feasible. Choosing algorithms that support longer key lengths ensures your data remains secure even in the long run.

Implementing Robust Key Management

- Secure Key Generation: The foundation of strong key management lies in unpredictable keys. Utilize cryptographically secure random number generators (CSPRNGs) to create random keys. These generators rely on algorithms that produce statistically unpredictable numbers, making it nearly impossible for attackers to guess the key.

- Hardware Security Modules (HSMs): HSMs are specialized hardware devices designed for the sole purpose of safeguarding cryptographic keys. They offer a robust layer of security with tamper-resistant enclosures, physical access controls, and secure key management functionalities. Consider HSMs for storing and managing encryption keys associated with highly sensitive data.

- Key Rotation Strategies: No key should remain static for an extended period. Establish a key rotation strategy that involves regularly changing your encryption keys. This reduces the window of opportunity for attackers who might exploit a compromised key. The frequency of key rotation depends on the sensitivity of the data and the potential consequences of a key breach.

Continuous Testing and Patch Management

- Proactive Vulnerability Assessments: Don't wait for a breach to discover vulnerabilities. Regularly conduct penetration testing and vulnerability scanning of your cryptographic implementations. These assessments can identify weaknesses in your code, libraries, or configurations that attackers might exploit.

- Patch Management Discipline: Software vendors regularly release security patches to address vulnerabilities in their products. Implement a rigorous patch management process to ensure all cryptographic libraries and software used within your systems are updated with the latest security patches promptly. This ensures that known vulnerabilities are addressed quickly, minimizing the risk of exploitation.

- Leveraging Open-Source Security: Consider using well-established open-source cryptographic libraries. The benefit of open-source lies in the transparency and scrutiny provided by a larger security community. Open-source libraries are often rigorously reviewed and patched promptly when vulnerabilities are discovered.

- Security Expertise Augmentation: Cryptography can be a complex field. Partnering with security professionals or managed security service providers (MSSPs) can provide access to specialized expertise. These experts can help you navigate the ever-changing threat landscape, select the most appropriate cryptographic solutions, and ensure their secure implementation.
- Staying Informed and Compliant: Regulatory requirements around data security are constantly evolving. Security professionals can help you stay informed about relevant regulations and ensure your cryptographic practices comply with industry standards and best practices.

Common Cryptographic Pitfalls

In the age of ubiquitous digital interactions, cryptography acts as a silent guardian in the background, scrambling sensitive data into an unreadable format. Imagine it as a high-tech secret code, shielding information traveling across networks from prying eyes. However, even the most sophisticated ciphers can falter, leaving data vulnerable to exploitation. Let's delve into the common pitfalls that can weaken your cryptographic defenses and explore strategies to fortify them.

Weak Encryption Algorithms

Just like relying on a flimsy lock to secure your house, using outdated or weak encryption algorithms offers little protection against determined attackers. These algorithms, with their limited key lengths and susceptibility to brute-force attacks, can be cracked with enough computing power, rendering the encrypted data vulnerable.

The first line of defense is employing encryption algorithms that are considered the gold standard in the cybersecurity industry. These algorithms, such as AES-256 for symmetric encryption and RSA with sufficient key lengths for asymmetric encryption, offer significantly stronger protection. However, the cybersecurity landscape is constantly evolving, so staying informed about the latest algorithm updates and best practices is crucial. Partner with security professionals to conduct regular reviews of your cryptographic practices to ensure you're leveraging the most effective algorithms for your specific needs.

Improper Key Management

Imagine losing the key to your treasure chest in cryptography, weak key management practices have a similar consequence. Inadequate practices, such as using weak passwords or storing keys on insecure devices, can expose your data. If an attacker manages to steal or guess your key, they can decrypt the data with ease, rendering encryption useless.

Remediation

Treat your cryptographic keys with the utmost importance they are the gatekeepers of your data's confidentiality. Implement robust key management practices that include:

- Secure Key Generation: Utilize cryptographically secure random number generators to create unpredictable keys. These generators rely on strong mathematical algorithms to produce random numbers that cannot be easily guessed or replicated by attackers.
- Fort Knox-Level Storage: Store your keys in Hardware Security Modules (HSMs) – tamper-resistant hardware devices specifically designed to safeguard cryptographic keys. HSMs offer a robust

layer of physical and logical security, protecting your keys from unauthorized access even in the event of a system breach.

- Regular Key Rotation: Regularly rotate your keys to minimize the window of opportunity for attackers who might try to exploit a compromised key. Key rotation intervals should be determined based on a risk assessment considering factors like the sensitivity of the data and the potential consequences of a key compromise.

Implementation Errors

Imagine a complex lock with a faulty internal mechanism, even the strongest materials can be bypassed. Similarly, errors in how cryptographic libraries or algorithms are implemented within software can introduce vulnerabilities that attackers can exploit. These errors might be unintentional bugs or even malicious code embedded by attackers. If left unaddressed, these flaws can create openings for attackers to gain unauthorized access to sensitive data.

Remediation

Proactive measures are crucial to mitigate the risk of implementation errors. Regularly test your cryptographic implementations for vulnerabilities using penetration testing tools or vulnerability scanners. Security researchers are constantly discovering new weaknesses, so keeping your cryptographic libraries and software up-to-date with the latest security patches is essential. This ensures that any known vulnerabilities are addressed promptly, keeping your data safe from evolving threats. When possible, consider using well-established and thoroughly vetted cryptographic libraries with a strong track record of security to minimize the risk of implementation errors. Leverage open-source libraries that benefit from the scrutiny of a larger security community.

By employing these additional considerations within each core best practice, you can create a multi-layered defense that significantly reduces the risk of cryptographic failures and safeguards your sensitive data in the digital age.

A03: Injection Attacks - Malicious Code Infiltration

Injection attacks represent a serious threat to the security of web applications. They involve malicious actors surreptitiously inserting harmful code into user inputs processed by the application. This code, when executed by the application, can lead to various adverse outcomes, including unauthorized data access, manipulation, or system compromise.

Analogous to a scenario where a baker diligently crafts a cake only to have an unknown individual introduce unwanted ingredients, injection attacks exploit vulnerabilities in the application's input processing mechanisms. Attackers capitalize on inadequately validated or sanitized inputs, injecting malicious code that the application unwittingly executes.

SQL injection is a prevalent form of injection attack, wherein attackers insert malicious SQL queries into input fields, potentially compromising the integrity and confidentiality of the underlying database. Additionally, Cross-Site Scripting (XSS) attacks involve injecting malicious scripts into web pages, posing risks such as session hijacking and data theft.

The ramifications of successful injection attacks can be severe, ranging from data breaches and financial losses to reputational damage for affected organizations. To mitigate these risks, developers must adopt robust input validation and sanitization practices. Techniques such as parameterized queries, prepared statements, and content security policies are crucial in preventing injection vulnerabilities.

Unveiling Injection Attacks - SQL Injection, XSS, etc.

Injection attacks are a prevalent threat lurking in the shadows of the web, targeting vulnerabilities in how web applications interact with various systems. These attacks involve the sneaky insertion of malicious code into user inputs, which then gets executed by the application, often with disastrous consequences. Here, we'll delve into three common types of injection attacks and the havoc they can wreak:

SQL Injection (SQLi)

SQL Injection (SQLi) stands as a notorious villain in the web security world. It preys on weaknesses in how applications interact with databases. Imagine a web application with a search bar that retrieves information from a database. If the application doesn't properly validate user input within the search bar, an attacker can inject malicious SQL code disguised as regular search terms. When the application executes this tampered search query, it unwittingly executes the attacker's SQL code on the database server. The consequences can be severe:

- Data Theft: Attackers can steal sensitive information like customer records, financial data, or even login credentials stored within the database.
- Data Manipulation: Malicious actors can modify or delete critical data, potentially causing disruptions to core functionalities of the application or even corrupting sensitive information.
- Unauthorized Access: In some cases, SQLi attacks can grant attackers unauthorized access to restricted areas of the application or even the underlying database server itself.

Remediation

- Input Validation and Sanitization: Implement robust input validation techniques to ensure user inputs conform to expected formats and don't contain malicious code. Sanitize user inputs by removing any potentially harmful characters before processing them.
- Parameterized Queries: Utilize parameterized queries, which separate data from SQL statements. This prevents user input from

being interpreted as SQL code, significantly reducing the risk of SQLi attacks.

- Least Privilege: Grant database users only the minimum privileges required to perform their designated tasks. This minimizes the potential damage if an attacker gains unauthorized access.

Cross-Site Scripting (XSS)

Cross-Site Scripting (XSS) attacks involve the injection of malicious scripts, typically JavaScript, into user-generated content on web pages. Think of a forum where users can post comments. If the application doesn't properly sanitize user input within the comment section, an attacker can embed malicious scripts within their comments. When unsuspecting users view the page containing the attacker's comment, the injected scripts are executed within their web browsers. This can lead to a variety of malicious activities:

- Session Hijacking: XSS attacks can be used to steal session cookies, allowing attackers to impersonate legitimate users and gain unauthorized access to their accounts.
- Phishing Attacks: Attackers can leverage XSS to redirect users to fraudulent websites designed to steal login credentials or other sensitive information.
- Website Defacement: In some cases, XSS attacks can be used to deface the website itself, vandalizing its content and damaging its reputation.

Remediation

- Input Encoding: Encode all user-generated content before displaying it on web pages. This ensures that any malicious scripts are rendered harmless and displayed as plain text. Common encoding techniques include HTML entity encoding and URL encoding.

- Output Sanitization: Sanitize user input before storing it in the database. This prevents the persistence of malicious scripts that could be executed later when the content is retrieved.
- Content Security Policy (CSP): Implement a Content Security Policy (CSP) to restrict the sources from which scripts can be loaded on your web pages. This helps mitigate XSS attacks by preventing attackers from injecting scripts from unauthorized sources.

Command Injection

Command Injection attacks take a different approach, injecting malicious operating system commands into user inputs. Imagine a web application that allows users to upload files. If the application doesn't validate or sanitize file names properly, an attacker can embed malicious commands within the filename itself. When the application processes the uploaded file, it might inadvertently execute the embedded commands on the server's operating system. This can have serious ramifications:

- System Compromise: Command Injection attacks can grant attackers complete control over the server, allowing them to install malware, steal data, or disrupt critical system processes.
- Unauthorized Access: Attackers can exploit these vulnerabilities to gain unauthorized access to sensitive resources on the server or even the entire network.
- Arbitrary Code Execution: In some cases, attackers can leverage Command Injection to execute arbitrary code on the server, giving them complete control over the system's functionalities.

Remediation

- Input Validation and Sanitization: Just like with SQLi, thoroughly validate, and sanitize user inputs to ensure they don't contain malicious commands or operating system code.

- Safe Functions: Use well-defined functions designed for specific tasks instead of relying on generic string manipulation functions when processing user input. This helps prevent unintended execution of operating system commands.

- Restrict File Uploads: Implement restrictions on file types that can be uploaded to your web application. This reduces the risk of attackers uploading files containing malicious code that could be executed through Command Injection vulnerabilities.

The Mechanics of Injection - How Attackers Exploit Vulnerabilities

We've explored the fundamental steps of injection attacks, but a deeper understanding lies in the specifics of how attackers craft their malicious code and how these attacks exploit different application functionalities. Here's a more granular look at each stage...

Malicious Payload Construction

- Reconnaissance and Targeting: Attackers are meticulous researchers. Before crafting their weapon, they meticulously probe the target application to identify its programming language, database type (if applicable), and potential injection points. This reconnaissance allows them to tailor the malicious code for maximum impact. It's like planning a heist – the more the attacker knows about the layout of the bank (the application), the security measures (validation), and the location of the vault (the database), the more effective their attack will be.

- Encoding for Deception: The malicious code itself is often cleverly disguised. Attackers leverage techniques like encoding and character escaping to bypass basic validation filters. Imagine a secret agent trying to sneak past a security checkpoint at an embassy. The agent might use a fake passport (encoded payload) to appear legitimate, hoping it blends in with real passports (valid user input) and avoids scrutiny.

- Leveraging Application Logic: A critical aspect of crafting effective injection payloads is aligning them with the application's logic. Attackers exploit how the application processes user input to achieve their goals. In SQL injection, for example, the attacker might construct a payload that modifies a legitimate SQL query to steal data. It's like a pickpocket who studies a person's routine (application logic) to know the opportune moment to strike (inject malicious code) and steal their wallet (sensitive data).

Bypassing the Gatekeeper

- Incomplete Validation Rules: Validation mechanisms are only as effective as the rules they enforce. If the rules don't account for all possible malicious input variations, attackers can exploit these gaps. For instance, simple validation that only checks for allowed characters might not catch cleverly encoded SQL queries. It's like having a security guard at a museum who only checks for backpacks (basic validation) – a determined thief could smuggle in a stolen artifact hidden inside a rolled-up poster (malicious payload that bypasses validation).
- Logical Flaws in Validation: Even seemingly robust validation rules can have logical flaws. Attackers can sometimes craft inputs that technically satisfy the validation criteria but still contain malicious code that exploits vulnerabilities within the application's logic. Imagine a complex combination lock on a bank vault (validation). A skilled thief might discover a specific sequence of numbers (crafted input) that technically unlocks the vault (passes validation) but gains unauthorized access through a flaw in the lock's mechanism (logical flaw in validation).
- Security Misconfigurations: Validation mechanisms can be bypassed if they're not properly configured. Developers might inadvertently disable certain security checks, leaving the application vulnerable to specific injection attacks. It's like leaving a back door unlocked (misconfigured security) even though the

main entrance has a deadbolt (basic validation). An attacker can easily exploit this oversight to gain entry.

Understanding Execution Environments

- SQL Injection Battleground: The Database Server: In SQL injection, the injected code becomes part of a database query. The attacker's payload manipulates this query to perform unauthorized actions. The database server then interprets and executes the modified query, potentially granting the attacker access to sensitive data or allowing them to manipulate the database itself. Imagine the attacker sneaking their malicious code (the weapon) into a legitimate SQL query (like an armoured Trojan horse). Once inside the database server (the battlefield), the code is executed, allowing the attacker to steal information or wreak havoc.

- XSS Playground: The User's Browser: Cross-Site Scripting attacks target the user's web browser. The injected malicious code, often JavaScript, is executed within the browser's environment. This code can then interact with the web page and steal user data, redirect users to phishing sites, or deface the website itself. Imagine the attacker planting malicious code in a seemingly harmless comment on a social media platform (XSS vulnerability). When unsuspecting users view the comment (the trigger), the code executes within their browser (the playground), potentially stealing their login credentials or redirecting them to fraudulent websites.

- Command Injection's Dark Alley: The Operating System: Command injection attacks exploit vulnerabilities that allow user input to be treated as operating system commands. When the application processes the attacker's input, it inadvertently executes these commands on the server's operating system. This can grant the attacker complete control over the server, allowing them to install malware, steal data, or disrupt critical system processes. It's like tricking the application into opening a command prompt (the dark alley) and unknowingly typing in commands crafted by the attacker (the weapon).

Understanding Attacker Objectives

We've explored how attackers craft their weapons and how these weapons exploit vulnerabilities within applications. Now, let's delve into the attacker's motives and the potential consequences of successful injection attacks...

- Data Exfiltration: A primary objective in many injection attacks, particularly SQL injection, is data theft. Attackers can use their injected code to extract sensitive information such as customer records, financial data, or user credentials stored within databases. This stolen data can then be sold on the black market or used for further malicious activities like identity theft or financial fraud.

- Maintaining Persistence: In some cases, attackers might leverage injection attacks to establish a foothold within the system. They can achieve this by planting additional malicious code, often referred to as backdoors, that allow them to maintain persistent access to the compromised system. This backdoor can then be used to launch further attacks, steal data over time, or deploy malware across the network.

- Lateral Movement and Privilege Escalation: Once attackers gain access to a system through an injection attack, they might attempt to move laterally within the network. This involves compromising additional systems or user accounts to expand their reach and control. Additionally, attackers might try to escalate their privileges within the compromised system, gaining access to more sensitive resources and potentially taking complete control of the server.

- Denial-of-Service (DoS) Attacks: While data theft is a common goal, injection attacks can also be used to disrupt the availability of a service. Attackers might craft malicious payloads that overload the database server with complex queries in SQL injection or exploit vulnerabilities to consume excessive resources in other injection attacks. This can render the targeted service unavailable to legitimate users, causing downtime and potential financial losses.

Safeguarding Against Injection with Secure Coding Practices

While the previous section explored some foundational practices, here's a deeper dive into advanced techniques that developers can leverage to create a comprehensive defense against injection attacks, turning your web application into a security fortress...

Input Validation

- Input Type Checking: Move beyond simple character validation and implement mechanisms to ensure user inputs conform to the expected data type. Imagine a bank teller meticulously examining a deposit slip. They wouldn't just look for typos; they'd verify that the amount field contains only numbers, and the account number adheres to a specific format. Similarly, enforce numerical input for fields that should only contain numbers (like quantity fields in an online store), and restrict text fields to alphanumeric characters or specific allowed symbols (like usernames that shouldn't include special characters).
- Regular Expressions for Granular Control: Regular expressions provide developers with a powerful tool to define precise patterns that valid user inputs must adhere to. Think of them as advanced filters, offering much more granular control compared to basic character checks. For instance, a regular expression can ensure that a username starts with a letter, contains only letters,

numbers, and underscores, and has a minimum and maximum length. This level of precision significantly reduces the likelihood of attackers sneaking malicious code disguised as valid user input.

- Whitelist vs Blacklist Approach: When deciding on a validation strategy, consider the trade-offs between whitelisting and blacklisting. A whitelist acts like a strict guard dog, only allowing users who provide specific, pre-defined inputs. This offers maximum security but can potentially limit functionality. For example, a whitelist might only allow usernames that match a specific format (e.g., alphanumeric characters and underscores). While highly secure, this could restrict users who want usernames with special characters or numbers. Conversely, a blacklist functions like a more lenient guard dog, explicitly denying certain malicious patterns while allowing everything else. This offers more flexibility but requires careful maintenance to stay up-to-date with evolving attack techniques. Imagine a blacklist that denies usernames containing script tags or SQL keywords often used in injection attacks. This would be effective, but new attack methods might emerge that the blacklist wouldn't catch. The choice between whitelisting and blacklisting depends on the specific application's needs and risk tolerance.

Parameterization

- Stored Procedures: Consider using stored procedures for complex database interactions. These pre-compiled procedures reside on the database server itself and enforce strict parameter definitions. Data and SQL code are kept entirely separate within stored procedures. This significantly reduces the risk of SQL injection since attackers cannot inject malicious code into the queries themselves. Imagine a well-fortified armoury where weapons (data) are stored separately from ammunition (SQL code). This makes it much harder for attackers to gain access to the weapons and use them for malicious purposes.

- Prepared Statements: For applications that don't utilize stored procedures, leverage prepared statements. These statements act as parameterized queries within the application code itself. When using a prepared statement, the developer defines the SQL query structure but leaves placeholders for the actual data values. These placeholders are then filled with the user-provided input later. Prepared statements offer similar protection against SQL injection as stored procedures by ensuring that data and code remain separate. Think of prepared statements as a secure way to pass instructions and ingredients (data) to the kitchen (database) without compromising the recipe (SQL code) itself.

Data Sanitization

- Context-Aware Sanitization: Data sanitization routines should be tailored to the specific context of the user input. Just as a baker might use different cleaning methods for raw ingredients compared to pre-washed vegetables, data going into a database field might require different sanitization procedures compared to data displayed on a web page. For instance, data entering a database field containing email addresses might involve removing any special characters that could disrupt the database query, while data displayed on a web page might require HTML entity encoding to ensure that any script tags or angle brackets within the user input are rendered harmless and displayed as plain text.
- Encoding for Safe Display: When displaying user-generated content on web pages, implement appropriate encoding techniques like HTML entity encoding or URL encoding. Imagine a shop owner carefully examining a customer's credit card before swiping it. Just because the card looks valid doesn't mean it can't be tampered with. Similarly, user-generated content might appear legitimate but could contain malicious code.
- Patch Management: Staying on top of security updates for all software components and libraries used within your application is

paramount. These updates often include patches for newly discovered vulnerabilities that attackers might try to exploit. Think of them as constantly reinforcing the walls of your fortress with the latest building materials and defensive measures. A single weak point in the wall can be a critical entry point for attackers. Regular patching ensures that these vulnerabilities are addressed promptly, minimizing the window of opportunity for attackers.

- Dependency Scanning: Many applications rely on third-party libraries and frameworks. While convenient, these external components can also introduce security risks if they contain vulnerabilities. Utilize dependency scanning tools to identify any known vulnerabilities within the third-party libraries your application depends on. Once identified, update the libraries to patched versions or find alternative libraries that are secure. Imagine conducting regular inspections of your fortress to identify any weaknesses, not just in the main walls but also in any drawbridges or gates (third-party components) that provide access.

Proactive Security Measures

- Security Code Reviews: Incorporate security code reviews as a standard practice within your development lifecycle. These reviews involve security experts or experienced developers scrutinizing the code for potential vulnerabilities, including injection points. Imagine having a team of security inspectors examine the blueprints and construction of your fortress before it's built, identifying any flaws in the design that could be exploited by attackers.
- Security Awareness Training: Educate not only developers but also security personnel and anyone involved in the application lifecycle about injection attacks and secure coding practices. The more everyone understands the threats and how to mitigate them, the stronger your overall security posture becomes. Think of this as

training your guards (developers and security personnel) on how to identify and defend against potential intruders (attackers) who might try to exploit weaknesses in your defenses.

By implementing these advanced techniques in conjunction with the foundational practices discussed earlier, developers can create a robust defense against injection attacks. Remember, security is an ongoing process that requires continuous vigilance and adaptation. As attackers develop new methods, so too must defenders refine their strategies. By staying informed, adopting a layered security approach, and fostering a culture of security within your development team, you can create a web application that is truly a Fort Knox against injection attacks.

A04: Insecure Design - Flawed Foundations

Imagine embarking on the construction of a magnificent palace nestled along the shoreline, envisioning its grandeur against the backdrop of the ocean. Yet, despite meticulous planning and intricate architectural designs, the foundation remains neglected. As the relentless tide encroaches, the unstable sands beneath the palace gradually erode, causing the once-promising structure to teeter and eventually crumble into the sea. This unfortunate scenario serves as a poignant metaphor for the perilous consequences of Insecure Design in the digital realm.

In the realm of software development, Insecure Design represents a fundamental flaw in the architectural blueprint of an application. While features and functionalities may dazzle users, the absence of a robust security framework compromises the integrity and resilience of the entire system. Just as a palace's stability hinges upon a solid foundation, the security of an application is contingent upon a design that prioritizes security from its inception.

A secure application begins with a comprehensive approach to design—one that integrates security considerations seamlessly into every phase of development. This proactive stance involves identifying and addressing potential security vulnerabilities at the outset, rather than attempting to retrofit security measures after the fact. By instilling security principles into the DNA of the application's architecture, developers can establish a resilient framework capable of withstanding the onslaught of malicious threats.

Insecure Design not only undermines the security posture of an application but also jeopardizes the trust and confidence of its users. Just as the eroding sands erode the foundation of the palace, vulnerabilities in the design of an application can lead to catastrophic breaches, data leaks, and system compromises. The consequences reverberate far beyond the digital realm, tarnishing reputations and inciting legal and financial repercussions.

Principles of Secure Design for Web Applications

While the previous section provided a foundational understanding of secure design principles, let's delve deeper into the reasoning and implications of each principle...

Security as a Priority

- Shifting the Mindset: Traditionally, security was often bolted onto applications as an afterthought. This reactive approach leaves applications vulnerable. Secure design flips this script, making security a core consideration from the get-go. Imagine building a palace – you wouldn't wait until the structure is complete to consider adding walls and a roof. Security needs to be part of the initial design and integrated throughout the development process.
- Long-Term Benefits: Prioritizing security from the outset yields significant benefits. Early security considerations can streamline the development process, avoiding costly rework later when vulnerabilities are discovered. Additionally, a secure foundation makes the application more robust and resilient against evolving threats. Just as a well-built palace can withstand the test of time, a securely designed application is less susceptible to future attacks.
- Integration with Development Practices: Secure design principles seamlessly integrate with established development methodologies like Agile or Waterfall. Security considerations can be incorporated into activities like threat modelling, code reviews, and security testing. This ensures that security is not a separate silo but rather a continuous thread woven into the entire development fabric.

- Understanding the Landscape: Threat modelling involves systematically identifying potential security threats that an application might face. Frameworks like STRIDE (Spoofing, Tampering, Repudiation, Information Disclosure, Denial-of-Service, Elevation of Privilege) provide a structured approach to analyze vulnerabilities. Imagine a security consultant meticulously examining the blueprints of the palace to identify weaknesses that attackers could exploit.

- Predictive Approach: By proactively identifying threats, developers can take steps to mitigate them early in the development process. This proactive approach is far more effective and less costly than scrambling to fix vulnerabilities after an application is deployed and potentially compromised. Just as the palace security team can address weaknesses in the walls before an attack, developers can address security flaws before they become exploitable.

- Considering Different Attackers: Threat modelling should consider various attacker profiles, from script kiddies with limited skills to sophisticated cybercriminals. Understanding the motivations and capabilities of different attackers helps developers prioritize which threats pose the greatest risk and allocate resources accordingly. Imagine the palace security plan considering threats from both petty thieves and well-organized heist attempts.

Defense in Depth

- Mitigating Single Points of Failure: Defense in depth is a security philosophy that advocates for employing multiple layers of security controls. This approach ensures that if one layer is breached, others remain in place to hinder attackers. Imagine a palace with a combination of security measures – sturdy walls, a moat, vigilant guards, and an alarm system. Even if an attacker breaches the wall (one layer), they still face other obstacles before reaching the treasure (sensitive data).

- Complementary Controls: The different security controls implemented in a defense-in-depth strategy should complement each other. For example, strong authentication mechanisms (like multi-factor authentication) can act as the first line of defense, while input validation and data encryption can provide additional layers of protection. Think of the palace guards working in tandem with the alarm system and the moat to create a comprehensive security net.
- Continuous Monitoring: Defense in depth doesn't stop at implementation. Security controls need to be continuously monitored and tested for effectiveness. Regular security assessments and penetration testing can identify potential weaknesses in the layered defenses. Imagine the palace guards regularly patrolling the grounds and conducting security drills to ensure their preparedness.

By understanding the reasoning behind these principles and their practical applications, developers can build web applications with a security-first mindset, creating a more robust and resilient digital fortress against ever-present cyber threats.

Identifying Insecure Design Flaws

We've explored some common design flaws that can introduce vulnerabilities into web applications. Now, let's delve deeper into the consequences of these flaws and how to address them effectively...

Balancing Security and Usability

- The Friction Paradox: Excessively complex authentication processes create friction for users, potentially leading them to adopt insecure practices like weak passwords or password sharing. Striking a balance between robust security and user-friendliness is crucial. Imagine an overly complex palace entry gate with multiple locks and riddles – it may deter legitimate visitors and even tempt them to sneak in through a back door (insecure practices).

- Usability Matters: Usability research can help developers design authentication mechanisms that are both secure and user-friendly. Multi-factor authentication (MFA) offers a strong security layer without overwhelming users, while password meters provide real-time feedback on password strength. Think of a well-designed palace entrance that incorporates modern security measures like key card access while still maintaining a welcoming atmosphere.

- Context-Aware Security: Tailor authentication complexity based on the sensitivity of the data or actions being accessed. Low-risk actions might necessitate simpler logins, while high-risk actions could require additional verification steps like MFA. Imagine the palace having a simple guard check for entry to the gardens but requiring a more rigorous security check for access to the treasury.

Lack of Input Validation

- The Injection Threat: Neglecting input validation opens the door for injection attacks. Attackers can inject malicious code into user inputs, potentially compromising the application's security. Imagine a palace with no guards to inspect incoming goods – attackers could easily smuggle in weapons (malicious code) disguised as harmless items (user input).

- Validation Best Practices: Implement robust input validation routines to ensure user inputs conform to expected formats and don't contain malicious code. Techniques like whitelisting or blacklisting can help filter out invalid or harmful inputs. Think of the palace guards meticulously examining incoming goods, verifying their authenticity, and ensuring they pose no threat.

- Data Sanitization: Even with validation, consider data sanitization to remove potentially harmful characters or code before processing user input. This adds an extra layer of defense. Imagine the palace guards not only checking goods but also disinfecting them to eliminate any potential hazards before bringing them inside.

Insecure Data Storage

- Encryption Essentials: Sensitive data such as passwords, financial information, or personal details must be encrypted using robust algorithms. Storing data in plain text is akin to leaving the palace treasure vault unlocked – a security nightmare. Imagine the palace treasury storing its riches (sensitive data) in unlocked chests – a prime target for thieves (attackers).
- Encryption at Rest and in Transit: Encrypt data not only at rest (on servers) but also in transit (during transmission). Think of the palace transporting its treasures in heavily guarded, armoured carriages (encryption) to prevent theft during transport.
- Key Management: Securely manage encryption keys to ensure they are not compromised. Imagine the palace having robust protocols for safeguarding the keys to the treasure vault – losing them would be catastrophic.

Insufficient Logging and Monitoring

- The Visibility Challenge: Without proper logging and monitoring, detecting suspicious activity or identifying security incidents becomes a significant challenge. This is akin to a palace lacking vigilant guards or any record of visitors – potential breaches or intrusions could go unnoticed. Imagine the palace having no guards patrolling the grounds and keeping no visitor logs – a recipe for disaster.

- Log Everything (Almost): Implement comprehensive logging practices to capture user activity, system events, and security-related incidents. However, be mindful of privacy regulations and only log essential data. Think of the palace guards meticulously documenting all activity within the palace grounds, but adhering to strict protocols regarding what information is recorded.
- Security Information and Event Management (SIEM): Utilize Security Information and Event Management (SIEM) solutions to aggregate and analyze log data from various sources, allowing for efficient detection of anomalies and potential security threats. Imagine the palace having a central command center that receives reports from all guards and analyzes them for any suspicious patterns or breaches.

By addressing these insecure design flaws and implementing the suggested security measures, developers can create a robust digital architecture that resembles a well-fortified palace. Through a user-centric approach to authentication, rigorous input validation, secure data storage practices, and comprehensive logging and monitoring, developers can build applications that are not only secure but also foster user trust and confidence.

Prioritizing Security Throughout the Development Lifecycle

Integrating security considerations throughout the development lifecycle is essential for creating a more secure and resilient application.

Security Champions - Threat Modelling with a Sharper Focus

Appointing security champions within the development team can greatly enhance security practices. These individuals advocate for secure design principles and serve as dedicated advisors, ensuring that security remains a priority throughout the development process. Like having a seasoned security advisor overseeing the planning of the palace construction, security champions guide the team in implementing robust security measures from the outset.

- Evolving Threat Modelling: While frameworks like STRIDE (Spoofing, Tampering, Repudiation, Information Disclosure, Denial-of-Service, Elevation of Privilege) provide a valuable foundation for threat modelling, consider incorporating attacker personas into the exercise. These personas represent different adversary profiles, ranging from opportunistic script kiddies with limited technical skills to well-funded, highly sophisticated cybercriminal organizations. Imagine the palace security team not just considering generic threats like theft, but also tailoring their defenses against potential infiltration attempts by cunning spies or well-equipped heist operations.

- Understanding the "Why" Behind the Attack: By understanding the motivations and capabilities of each attacker persona, developers can prioritize security threats more effectively and allocate resources accordingly. For instance, a script kiddie might focus on exploiting readily available vulnerabilities using automated tools, while a state-sponsored attacker might employ more sophisticated zero-day exploits or social engineering techniques. The palace guards would likely prioritize securing the treasure vault (critical data) with more robust access control systems and vigilant patrols compared to the kitchens (less critical data) that might rely on simpler measures.

- Targeted Mitigations for Stronger Defenses: Develop targeted mitigation strategies for each attacker persona identified during threat modelling. This allows for a more nuanced approach to security, focusing on the most likely threats posed by specific attacker types. Imagine the palace implementing advanced biometric authentication systems and laser security grids for the vault (against sophisticated attackers) while using swipe card access control for less sensitive areas like administrative offices.

Regular security reviews conducted throughout the development lifecycle are crucial for identifying and addressing potential vulnerabilities. These reviews involve scrutinizing code, architecture, and design choices to uncover any security flaws or weaknesses. Just as having palace blueprints reviewed by expert architects ensures structural integrity, conducting security reviews ensures that the application's architecture is resilient against cyber threats.

- Leveraging Static Code Analysis (SCA) Tools for Early Detection: While secure coding practices are an essential foundation for building secure applications, static code analysis (SCA) tools can significantly enhance the development process by automating the detection of common vulnerabilities within the codebase. These tools can identify potential security issues early in the development cycle, saving time and resources that would otherwise be spent manually searching for vulnerabilities. Imagine the palace security team using blueprints with built-in structural integrity checks to identify weaknesses before construction begins, rather than relying solely on visual inspections after the foundation is laid.

- Dependency Management with Security in Mind: Many modern applications rely on third-party libraries and frameworks to achieve desired functionalities. While these dependencies can be advantageous for development efficiency, they can also introduce security vulnerabilities if not managed properly. Implement a robust dependency management strategy that includes vulnerability scanning to identify known security weaknesses within the third-party components your application uses. Additionally, stay up-to-date with security patches released by vendors to ensure these dependencies don't become chinks in your application's security Armor. Think of the palace ensuring all building materials and tools used in construction come from reputable vendors with good security track records, and that these materials are regularly inspected for potential flaws.

- Security Champions as Code Review Partners: Security champions can play a vital role in code reviews by not only focusing on general functionality but also scrutinizing code for adherence to secure coding best practices. This collaborative approach between developers and security champions can significantly improve the overall security posture of the application. Imagine the palace security advisor participating in construction reviews alongside the architects and engineers, providing valuable insights not just on structural integrity but also on the security of entry points, guard posts, and other security measures.

- Security Information and Event Management (SIEM) for Threat Detection: SIEM tools are powerful for aggregating and analyzing security logs from various sources within your IT infrastructure, including the deployed application. These tools can help identify suspicious activity, potential security incidents, and emerging threats by correlating events and identifying patterns that might otherwise be missed. Imagine the palace having a central command center that collects data from guards, alarms, CCTV footage, and other sensors to identify any suspicious behaviour or potential breaches in real-time.

- Vulnerability Management Programs for Proactive Defense: Establish a program for proactively identifying and patching vulnerabilities in deployed applications. This includes subscribing to security advisories from vendors of the technologies you use, and regularly scanning your application for known vulnerabilities using security testing tools. Think of the palace guards constantly being trained on new attack methods and the palace itself being inspected and upgraded periodically to address any emerging security weaknesses discovered through intelligence gathering or security audits.

- Incident Response Planning: Preparing for the Unexpected: Even with the most comprehensive security measures in place, the possibility of a security breach can never be eliminated. Therefore, it's crucial to be prepared for such an eventuality. Develop a comprehensive incident response plan that outlines the steps to take in case of a security breach. This plan should define roles and responsibilities, communication protocols, and procedures for investigation, containment, eradication, and recovery. Imagine the palace having a well-rehearsed emergency response plan in case of an intrusion attempt, including protocols for alerting guards, evacuating residents, and apprehending attackers, while also having a plan to recover stolen items and repair any damage caused.

- Incident response drills: Conduct regular incident response drills to test the effectiveness of your plan and identify areas for improvement. Just as the palace guards would conduct practice drills to ensure their preparedness for various security scenarios, regular testing of the incident response plan helps identify weaknesses and ensures a smooth and coordinated response during an actual security breach.

Security Testing

Security testing serves as a cornerstone in the development lifecycle, safeguarding applications from potential breaches before they occur. By simulating real-world attack scenarios, security testing unearths vulnerabilities that could be exploited by malicious actors. Let's delve deeper into this critical realm and explore the various techniques that work in tandem to fortify your application's defenses.

Unveiling Weaknesses

- Static Application Security Testing (SAST): Imagine a security inspector meticulously examining blueprints. SAST operates in a similar fashion, meticulously analyzing the application's code itself. Its keen eye searches for vulnerabilities like SQL injection, cross-site scripting (XSS), and insecure direct object references the common chinks in the Armor that attackers can exploit to manipulate data or gain unauthorized access.

- Dynamic Application Security Testing (DAST): DAST goes beyond static analysis, transforming from blueprint inspector to a security inspector actively testing the running application. Testers strategically probe the application with various inputs, mimicking the manoeuvres of a determined attacker. This dynamic approach helps identify vulnerabilities that might remain concealed during static analysis, ensuring a more comprehensive security assessment.

- Penetration Testing (Pen Testing): Envision a team of security consultants meticulously planning an attack. Pen testing embodies this scenario, deploying ethical hackers who employ various techniques to discover exploitable weaknesses. These skilled individuals attempt to infiltrate the application's defenses, mimicking the methods and tools used by real-world attackers. Pen testing provides an in-depth evaluation of the application's security posture, uncovering vulnerabilities that might evade automated testing tools and offering invaluable insights for shoring up defenses.

- Security Scanning: Security scanning tools function as automated sentries, continuously patrolling the application for signs of trouble. These tools can encompass vulnerability scanning, configuration assessments, and more. By integrating security scans throughout the development lifecycle, organizations can proactively identify potential security issues early on, nipping them in the bud before they blossom into full-fledged vulnerabilities.

The Benefits of a Proactive Approach

- Proactive Vulnerability Identification: Security testing's core strength lies in its ability to unearth vulnerabilities before they can be actively exploited by attackers. This proactive approach saves organizations significant time, resources, and reputational damage in the event of a security breach. Imagine patching a leaky roof before a storm instead of scrambling to repair the damage afterward – security testing allows you to address weaknesses before they are exposed to a real attack.

- Building a Robust Security Posture: By diligently addressing the vulnerabilities unearthed during security testing, organizations can significantly bolster the overall security posture of their applications. This enhanced security makes it exponentially more difficult for attackers to gain unauthorized access to sensitive data or disrupt critical systems. Think of a medieval castle being fortified with stronger walls, additional guards, and improved weaponry. Security testing helps your application achieve a similar level of resilience against modern digital threats.

- Enhanced Confidence and Trust: Regular security testing goes beyond technical measures; it demonstrates a commitment to security that fosters trust with users and stakeholders. When users know that an application undergoes rigorous security testing, they are more likely to feel secure providing their personal information or using the application. Imagine feeling safe entering a well-lit, well-guarded building compared to a dimly lit, seemingly abandoned one. Security testing assures users that your application is a safe space for their data.

Strategically integrating a combination of these security testing techniques throughout the development lifecycle, organizations can construct a multi-layered security fortress. This comprehensive approach empowers them to create applications that are not only functionally sound but also inherently more secure and resilient against the ever-evolving landscape of cyber threats. Remember, security testing is an ongoing endeavour, not a one-time event. By consistently testing and improving your application's defenses, you can ensure its continued security in the face of persistent digital adversaries.

A05: Security Misconfiguration - Unintended Openings

Imagine a magnificent castle with sturdy walls and a strong gate, but a single, unlocked window on the ground floor. This vulnerability, akin to Security Misconfiguration, can compromise the security of an entire application. Misconfigured systems create unintended openings that attackers can exploit to gain unauthorized access or disrupt operations.

The Importance of Secure System Configuration

Secure system configuration is paramount for web applications, which operate within complex ecosystems of diverse software components and servers, each governed by unique configuration settings. These configurations define critical aspects of system functionality, including security controls, access permissions, and error handling. Like a well-maintained castle relying on vigilant guards and secure locks to safeguard its inhabitants, a secure application depends on meticulous system configuration.

A solid foundation of secure system configuration serves as the bedrock upon which the entire application security posture rests. It encompasses a wide range of settings, from authentication mechanisms to encryption protocols, establishing robust defenses against a variety of cyber threats. By configuring these parameters meticulously, developers establish a strong framework for defending against potential security breaches and vulnerabilities.

Proper system configuration is essential for mitigating risks associated with unauthorized access and data breaches. Stringent access controls and robust authentication mechanisms help thwart unauthorized entry, while fine-tuned error handling and logging configurations enable swift detection and response to security incidents. Implementing secure configurations minimizes the impact of security breaches on the application and its users.

Secure system configuration also plays a crucial role in ensuring compliance with regulatory requirements and industry standards. Many regulatory frameworks mandate specific security configurations to protect sensitive data and mitigate cyber risks. By adhering to these standards and implementing secure configurations, organizations demonstrate their commitment to data protection and regulatory compliance.

Common Security Misconfigurations in Web Applications

Web applications offer a plethora of features and conveniences, but security misconfigurations can introduce critical vulnerabilities. These misconfigurations act as chinks in the armour, creating openings that attackers can exploit to gain unauthorized access, disrupt operations, or steal sensitive data. Let's delve deeper into some of the most prevalent security misconfigurations that web applications face...

Default Configurations

Many applications arrive pre-configured with settings that prioritize ease of use over ironclad security. This creates a tempting target for attackers who are familiar with these common defaults and exploit them if they remain unchanged after deployment. Imagine a majestic castle equipped with factory-made locks, all sharing the same key! An attacker, aware of this default setting, can easily gain unauthorized access, just like someone possessing the master key to the entire castle.

To mitigate this risk, developers should move away from default configurations and implement security best practices from the outset. This may involve setting strong, unique passwords, disabling unnecessary features, and adhering to the principle of least privilege, which grants users only the minimal access required for their tasks.

Unnecessary Services

Leaving unnecessary services or functionalities enabled on a web application introduces additional attack vectors. These services act like hidden passages within a castle, unknown to the guards. Malicious actors can exploit these unnoticed features to gain access to the system and wreak havoc.

A systematic approach to hardening web servers and applications is essential to address this vulnerability. This involves identifying and disabling any services or functionalities that are not critical for the core operation of the application. By removing these extraneous features, you eliminate potential backdoors that attackers could use to infiltrate the system.

Weak Permissions

Improperly configured access controls can inadvertently grant unauthorized users access to sensitive data or functionalities within a web application. Imagine castle guards who allow anyone dressed in a vaguely similar uniform to enter restricted areas. Weak permissions represent a similar security lapse, compromising the effectiveness of the application's security measures. Just as a castle with lax entry protocols is vulnerable, weak permissions can expose sensitive data and functionalities to unauthorized individuals.

The principle of least privilege offers a powerful defense against weak permissions. By adhering to this principle, developers can ensure that users and applications have only the minimal level of access required to perform their designated tasks. This minimizes the potential damage that can be caused by a compromised account or a malicious actor exploiting weak permissions.

Outdated Software

Operating a web application with outdated software containing known vulnerabilities creates exploitable entry points for attackers. This is akin to a castle relying on a weak, rusty gate that's easy to break down. Outdated software with unpatched vulnerabilities presents a significant security risk, leaving the application susceptible to various attacks and potential compromise.

Regular patch management is crucial to address this vulnerability. Developers and system administrators must stay up-to-date on the latest security patches for all software components and libraries used within the web application. Promptly installing these patches ensures that known vulnerabilities are addressed, effectively closing the gaps in the application's defenses.

Hardening Web Servers and Applications

While security misconfigurations can create vulnerabilities, developers and system administrators are not powerless. Here's an arsenal of proactive measures to fortify your web application castle and minimize the risk of attacks...

Security Hardening

Security hardening is a systematic approach, akin to reinforcing the castle walls, installing stronger locks, and eliminating hidden passages. It involves meticulously reviewing and adjusting security settings on web servers and applications. This can encompass actions like...

- Disabling unused protocols and services.
- Configuring strong access controls.
- Enabling logging and security monitoring.
- Utilizing firewalls and intrusion detection systems.

By implementing security hardening practices, you create a more robust defense system for your web application, making it significantly more challenging for attackers to exploit weaknesses.

Least Privilege Principle

The least privilege principle dictates that users and applications should only be granted the minimum level of access required to perform their designated tasks. Imagine castle guards issuing specific keys to authorized personnel based on their duties.

- System administrators have elevated access for configuration purposes.
- Content editors only need access to modify specific content areas.

This approach minimizes potential damage if an account is compromised. Even if an attacker gains unauthorized access, their limited privileges restrict their ability to cause significant harm.

Disable Unnecessary Services

Many web applications have features or services enabled by default that might not be essential for core functionalities. These act like hidden passages within a castle, unknown to the guards, and can provide attackers with avenues for exploitation.

- Identify any unused services or functionalities.
- Disable or remove them if they are not critical for the application.

By eliminating these unnecessary features, you effectively seal off potential backdoors that attackers could use to infiltrate the system. This reduces the attack surface and strengthens the overall security posture of your web application.

Regular Patch Management

Running outdated software with known vulnerabilities is akin to a castle relying on a weak, rusty gate. Attackers can easily exploit these vulnerabilities to gain access. Here's how to stay vigilant:

- Implement a regular patching schedule for all software components and libraries used within the web application.
- Stay informed about the latest security patches and prioritize their installation.

By keeping software up-to-date, you address known vulnerabilities and effectively close the gaps in the application's defenses. This continuous process ensures your web application remains resilient against evolving cyber threats.

Security Monitoring

Proactive security monitoring involves scrutinizing system logs for any signs of suspicious activity. Imagine castle guards actively patrolling the grounds and reporting any unusual occurrences. Security monitoring allows you to...

- Identify potential attempts to exploit misconfigurations.
- Detect and respond to security incidents before they escalate.

By implementing security monitoring tools and procedures, you gain the ability to identify and address security issues promptly, minimizing the potential damage caused by misconfigurations.

Remember, security is an ongoing process. Continuous vigilance, secure configurations, up-to-date software, and a commitment to best practices are essential for building a robust and secure web application castle, capable of withstanding the ever-evolving threats of the digital world.

A06: Outdated Components - A Recipe for Risk

Imagine a magnificent palace built centuries ago, boasting exquisite architecture. However, the foundation crumbles due to age and neglect, putting the entire structure at risk. This scenario exemplifies the danger of Outdated Components in the digital world. Web applications are intricate ecosystems that rely on various software components and libraries. When these components become outdated and are not updated with the latest security patches, they introduce vulnerabilities that attackers can exploit.

The Peril of Vulnerable and Outdated Components

There are several reasons why outdated components pose a security risk...

- Known Vulnerabilities: Security researchers constantly discover vulnerabilities in software. Once a vulnerability is known, attackers can develop exploits to target those weaknesses. Outdated components often lack the security patches that address these vulnerabilities, leaving them wide open for attack. Imagine cracks appearing in the foundation and walls of the palace due to age, making it more susceptible to collapse.

- Limited Vendor Support: Software vendors typically cease providing security updates and bug fixes for older versions of their products. This means outdated components become increasingly susceptible to new threats as time progresses. Imagine the architects who built the palace centuries ago no longer being available to repair structural issues.

- Compatibility Issues: Integrating newer, more secure components with a legacy system can be challenging due to compatibility issues. This can create a situation where developers are forced to choose between functionality and security. Imagine trying to reinforce the palace foundation with modern materials that may not seamlessly integrate with the existing architecture.

Patch Management Strategies for Web Applications

Outdated software components harbour known vulnerabilities, creating exploitable entry points for attackers. Here are some effective strategies developers and system administrators can leverage to implement robust patch management and safeguard their web applications.

Regular Patch Management

Establish a systematic process for identifying, acquiring, and deploying security patches. Imagine a team of experts routinely inspecting the castle foundation, walls, and roof for weaknesses and promptly addressing any issues they discover. Regular patch management involves...

- Scheduling regular patch scans to identify vulnerable components.
- Prioritizing and obtaining security patches from vendors.
- Developing and executing a plan for deploying patches in a timely manner.
- Testing patches in a non-production environment to minimize disruption.

By implementing a regular patch management process, you proactively address vulnerabilities before attackers can exploit them. This ensures your web application remains resilient against evolving cyber threats.

Software Bill of Materials (SBOM)

Maintain a comprehensive list of all software components used within your web application. This SBOM (Software Bill of Materials) should include details like version numbers and any known vulnerabilities associated with each component. Think of it as a detailed blueprint that identifies all building materials used in the palace construction. Having an SBOM offers several advantages...

- Improved visibility into the application's software ecosystem.

- Enables proactive identification of potential vulnerabilities within components.
- Facilitates targeted patching efforts by focusing on components with known risks.

A well-maintained SBOM empowers you to manage vulnerabilities effectively and prioritize remediation efforts based on potential impact.

Vulnerability Scanning

Conduct regular vulnerability scans of your web application and its underlying systems. These scans act like inspections performed by experts to identify any structural weaknesses within the palace. Vulnerability scanning tools can help detect...

- Outdated software components with known vulnerabilities.
- Misconfigurations that could be exploited by attackers.
- Other potential security weaknesses within the application environment.

By proactively identifying vulnerabilities through regular scans, you can prioritize patching efforts and address security risks before they are exploited.

Component Lifecycle Management

Develop a plan for updating or replacing outdated components as needed. This may involve migrating to newer, more secure versions or implementing workarounds to mitigate known vulnerabilities within older components. Imagine the palace undergoing renovations to strengthen the foundation and replace outdated materials with more secure alternatives. Here are some key considerations:

- Stay informed about the lifecycles of software components used in your application.

- Develop a strategy for migrating to newer versions or implementing alternative solutions.
- Carefully evaluate the risks and benefits of continuing to use outdated components.

By implementing a component lifecycle management plan, you ensure your web application leverages the latest security features and minimizes the risk associated with outdated components.

Maintaining Third-Party Libraries

The contemporary web application landscape thrives on the efficiency and functionality offered by third-party libraries. However, integrating these libraries necessitates a vigilant approach to security, akin to safeguarding the supply chain during palace renovations. Here, we explore strategies to ensure the security of third-party libraries within your web application...

Meticulous Security Reviews

Before incorporating any external library, a comprehensive security review is paramount. This process mirrors the rigorous inspection of building materials sourced from external suppliers before construction commences. Here's a breakdown of a robust security review...

- Automated Vulnerability Scans: Leverage automated tools to identify known vulnerabilities within the library codebase.
- Code Review (when feasible): Conduct a comprehensive code review to assess the overall security posture of the library's source code.
- Vendor Reputation Research: Investigate the vendor's track record for security practices. Do they exhibit a commitment to prompt security patch issuance and timely vulnerability remediation within their libraries?

By conducting a thorough security review, you gain valuable insights into potential security risks associated with the library. This empowers you to make informed decisions regarding its integration into your web application.

Prioritizing Security

The security landscape of third-party libraries is constantly evolving. You may encounter situations where a critical library falls short in these aspects...

- Active Maintenance: The library is no longer actively maintained by the vendor, potentially leaving it vulnerable to exploitation.
- Unresolved Vulnerabilities: The library harbours significant vulnerabilities that haven't been addressed by the vendor.

In such scenarios, consider these alternative strategies...

- Identifying Secure Alternatives: Seek out alternative libraries with a demonstrably strong security posture and active maintenance from reputable vendors.
- Developing Your Own Library: If no suitable alternative exists, and the library's functionality is crucial to your application, consider developing a secure in-house implementation.
- While prioritizing security might necessitate additional effort, it safeguards the long-term integrity of your application's codebase and minimizes the risk of vulnerabilities introduced by outdated or insecure libraries.

Additional Security Considerations

- Version Control: Always utilize a specific version of a library, avoiding reliance on the "latest" version by default. This allows you to maintain control over potential security implications introduced by newer versions.

- Dependency Management: Implement a dependency management tool to meticulously track all third-party libraries used within your application. This streamlines the update process and ensures you're notified of any security vulnerabilities discovered in the libraries you rely on.

By adhering to these strategies, you can effectively manage the security of third-party libraries and construct more secure web applications. Remember, a secure development lifecycle encompasses not just the security of your own code, but also the security of the external components that your application depends upon.

A07: Identification and Authentication Failures - The Broken Gate

Consider a majestic castle standing tall, fortified with imposing walls, and crowned with a magnificent gate, symbolizing strength and security. Yet, within this grandeur lies a critical flaw—the guards stationed at the gate are fast asleep, oblivious to the looming threat. As a result, anyone, friend, or foe, can simply stroll past the gate unchallenged, breaching the castle's defenses with ease.

This scenario vividly illustrates the vulnerabilities associated with Identification and Authentication Failures in the digital domain. In the intricate landscape of web applications, robust identification and authentication mechanisms serve as the modern-day gatekeepers. Their primary role is to discern friend from foe, granting access only to authorized individuals while repelling malicious actors.

Just as the vigilant guards should scrutinize each approaching visitor before granting entry to the castle, robust identification mechanisms verify the identity of users attempting to access digital resources. These mechanisms often involve the use of credentials, such as usernames and passwords, biometric data, or cryptographic keys, to authenticate users' identities.

Authentication, however, is only part of the equation. Much like the guards' awareness of who should be granted entry into the castle, robust identification processes must be complemented by effective authorization mechanisms. Authorization ensures that authenticated users have the appropriate permissions to access specific resources or perform certain actions within the application.

When Identification and Authentication mechanisms fail, it's akin to the guards at the castle gate being fast asleep. Unauthorized individuals can gain unfettered access to sensitive information, manipulate functionalities, or wreak havoc within the application. The consequences can be dire, ranging from data breaches and financial losses to reputational damage and legal repercussions.

To mitigate the risk of Identification and Authentication Failures, developers must implement robust security measures. This includes employing multifactor authentication, enforcing strong password policies, implementing session management best practices, and incorporating biometric authentication where feasible.

Implementing Secure Authentication Mechanisms (MFA, etc.)

Gone are the days of a single password being sufficient. Modern applications require a layered approach to authentication, incorporating multiple factors to verify a user's identity. Here are some common methods...

- Multi-Factor Authentication (MFA): This adds an extra layer of security by requiring users to provide multiple pieces of evidence beyond just a password. This could be a fingerprint scan, a security code sent to their phone, or a hardware token. Imagine the castle requiring not just a key (password), but also a specific voice recognition (fingerprint scan) and a physical token (security code) to gain entry.
- Strong Password Policies: Enforce strong password policies that mandate a minimum length, complexity requirements (uppercase, lowercase, numbers, symbols), and regular password changes. Think of the castle guards issuing strong, unique keys to authorized personnel and requiring them to be changed frequently.
- Single Sign-On (SSO): While convenient, single sign-on systems (SSO) can introduce a single point of failure. Implement additional security measures like MFA even when using SSO. Imagine having a single, heavily fortified gate for the castle, but also employing vigilant guards and additional security checks within the castle itself.

Thwarting Common Authentication Attacks

Attackers constantly devise methods to bypass authentication mechanisms:

- Brute-Force Attacks: Attackers use automated tools to try many password combinations until they crack the user's login credentials. Think of someone rapidly trying every key they can find to open the castle gate.
- Credential Stuffing: Attackers leverage stolen usernames and passwords from data breaches on other platforms to attempt logins on your application. Imagine someone trying keys stolen from other castles to open your castle gate.

Effective countermeasures include...

- Account Lockouts: Automatically lock user accounts after a certain number of failed login attempts to prevent brute-force attacks. Imagine the castle gate automatically locking after a set number of incorrect key attempts.
- Rate Limiting: Limit the number of login attempts allowed within a specific timeframe to hinder automated attacks. Think of the castle guards implementing a system to limit the number of attempted entries within a certain period.
- Password Hashing: Store passwords securely using a one-way hashing function. This ensures even if attackers gain access to the database, they cannot easily decipher the actual passwords. Imagine the castle storing a complex code derived from the key instead of the actual key itself.

Session Management Best Practices

Once a user has successfully navigated through the authentication process, ensuring robust session management practices becomes imperative to uphold the confidentiality and integrity of their interactions with the application. Here are the fundamental measures...

Session Timeouts

Implementing automatic session timeouts is crucial to proactively manage user sessions. By defining a period of inactivity after which users are automatically logged out, the risk of unauthorized access is significantly reduced. Just as vigilant castle guards would escort guests out after a certain duration of inactivity to maintain security, session timeouts serve as a proactive measure against potential threats in the digital realm.

Secure Session Tokens

Employing secure session tokens adds an extra layer of protection to user sessions. These tokens, which act as unique identifiers for authenticated sessions, should be designed to be resistant to forgery or hijacking attempts. Additionally, implementing token expiration mechanisms ensures that even if a token is compromised, its validity is limited. Analogous to the castle issuing temporary badges to authorized personnel, secure session tokens grant access privileges while minimizing the risk of unauthorized entry.

HTTPS Encryption

Enforcing HTTPS communication is essential to secure data transmission between the user's browser and the application server. By encrypting sensitive information, such as login credentials and session tokens, HTTPS prevents interception by malicious entities during transit. Visualize the establishment of a secure tunnel (HTTPS) between the user and the castle, ensuring that communication channels remain impervious to eavesdropping or tampering attempts.

By diligently adhering to these session management best practices, web applications can fortify their security posture, mitigate the risk of unauthorized access, and uphold the confidentiality of user data.

A08: Software and Data Integrity Failures - Broken Trust

Imagine a magnificent palace renowned for its exquisite treasures. However, if anyone could tamper with these treasures undetected, their value and authenticity would be severely compromised.

Software integrity encompasses the assurance that software components, including code and executables, remain unaltered and free from corruption throughout their lifecycle. Any unauthorized modifications to these components can introduce vulnerabilities or compromise the application's functionality, potentially leading to system instability or security breaches.

Similarly, data integrity involves guaranteeing the accuracy and reliability of stored data within the application. Protecting data integrity is vital, especially for sensitive information such as financial records or personal details, where even minor discrepancies can have significant consequences.

To mitigate the risk of Software and Data Integrity Failures, robust security measures must be implemented at every stage of the application's development and deployment. This includes techniques such as code signing and checksum verification to validate software integrity, implementing access controls and encryption to protect data from unauthorized tampering, and establishing stringent auditing and monitoring mechanisms to detect and respond to any suspicious activity promptly.

Safeguarding Data Integrity Throughout the Application Lifecycle

Data integrity refers to the accuracy and completeness of information throughout its lifecycle, from creation to storage and transmission. Here are some principles to ensure data integrity…

- Input Validation: Rigorously validate all user inputs to ensure they conform to expected formats and don't contain malicious code. Think of the palace guards meticulously inspecting any incoming items to ensure they are not tampered with.

- Data Validation: Implement mechanisms to verify the integrity of data at various stages, such as during storage, retrieval, and transmission. Imagine the palace having a system to confirm the authenticity and condition of the treasures upon arrival, storage, and retrieval.

- Data Encryption: Encrypt sensitive data at rest and in transit to prevent unauthorized access and modification. Imagine the palace storing its treasures in secure vaults with robust encryption measures.

- Data Backups: Maintain regular backups of data to ensure recovery in case of accidental or malicious modifications. Imagine the palace having copies of the treasures stored in secure locations for disaster recovery purposes.

The Impact of Data Integrity Failures

The consequences of data breaches and data integrity failures can be severe...

- Compromised User Information: Attackers can exploit vulnerabilities to steal or modify sensitive user data, such as financial information or personal details.

- Disrupted Operations: Tampered data can lead to system malfunctions, operational disruptions, and financial losses.

- Loss of Trust: Data breaches can erode user trust in an application and damage its reputation.

- Input Validation and Data Sanitization Techniques: Building Robust Defenses

Developers can employ various techniques to prevent unauthorized data modification...

- Input Validation: As discussed in Chapter 3 (Injection Attacks), rigorously validate all user inputs to ensure they are in the expected format and don't contain malicious code that could manipulate data.
- Data Sanitization: Sanitize all user inputs by removing any potentially harmful characters or code before processing them. Think of the palace guards carefully inspecting incoming items and removing any suspicious elements before they reach the treasures.
- Parameterized Queries: When interacting with databases, use parameterized queries to separate data from code, preventing SQL injection attacks that could modify database content (covered in earlier section- Injection Attacks). Imagine the palace having a secure system for registering new treasures that doesn't rely on users directly interacting with the vault itself.

Secure Coding Practices to Prevent Data Tampering

Data, within a web application, is akin to the precious treasures stored within a palace vault. Just as the palace implements security measures to safeguard its valuables, secure coding practices are essential to prevent attackers from tampering with data in your web application. Here, we explore some key strategies...

Input Validation and Sanitization

Input validation and sanitization are critical practices that function as the initial line of defense against data tampering. Imagine meticulous procedures for registering and retrieving treasures from the palace vault. Similarly...

- Input Validation: Rigorously validate all user input to ensure it conforms to expected data types and formats. This prevents malicious code injection attempts that could manipulate data.
- Input Sanitization: Sanitize all user input by removing or escaping any potentially harmful characters that could be exploited by attackers. This ensures only safe data enters your application.

By implementing robust input validation and sanitization practices, you significantly reduce the risk of attackers injecting malicious code or manipulating data within your application.

Error Handling

Even the most secure systems can encounter unexpected errors. Error handling mechanisms play a crucial role in preventing these errors from corrupting data within your web application. Imagine the palace having a well-defined system for handling any unforeseen events or mishaps during treasure registration or retrieval...

- Implement comprehensive error handling routines. These routines should gracefully handle unexpected errors and prevent system crashes that could potentially lead to data corruption.
- Log errors for further investigation. By logging errors, you gain valuable insights into potential issues within your application and can take steps to prevent them from recurring.
- Effective error handling ensures that even if unexpected situations arise, the integrity of your data remains protected.

Secure Coding Standards

Secure coding standards and best practices provide a strong foundation for secure application development. Imagine the palace architects and builders adhering to well-established construction principles to ensure the structural integrity of the treasure vault. Similarly...

- Adopt and adhere to industry-recognized secure coding standards. These standards provide guidance on best practices for writing secure code and minimizing the introduction of vulnerabilities.
- Train developers on secure coding principles. Equipping your development team with the necessary knowledge empowers them to write code that is less prone to security weaknesses.

By following secure coding standards and best practices, you cultivate a development environment that prioritizes security from the outset. This proactive approach significantly reduces the risk of vulnerabilities that could be exploited for data tampering purposes.

A09: Security Logging and Monitoring Failures

Imagine a magnificent palace with guards patrolling the grounds, but no record of their activities or any security cameras to monitor suspicious behaviour. This scenario exemplifies the dangers of Security Logging and Monitoring Failures. Without proper logging and monitoring, security incidents can go undetected, allowing attackers to operate freely within an application.

The Significance of Security Logging and Monitoring

Security logging and monitoring are crucial aspects of any robust security strategy. They provide valuable insights into system activity, allowing us to detect suspicious behaviour, identify potential threats, and investigate security incidents effectively. Think of the palace guards meticulously recording their patrols, noting any unusual occurrences, and having a system to review these logs to identify any potential security breaches.

What to Log for Effective Security Analysis: Capturing Crucial Information

Effective security logging captures a variety of information, including:

- User Activity: Track user logins, access attempts, and actions performed within the application. Imagine the palace guards logging who entered, when they entered, and what areas they accessed.

- System Events: Monitor system events like application errors, security warnings, and suspicious activity. Imagine the palace guards recording any strange noises, unusual movements, or malfunctioning security systems.

- Network Traffic: Monitor network traffic for anomalies that might indicate unauthorized access attempts or data exfiltration. Imagine the palace guards keeping track of any suspicious visitors or unauthorized attempts to enter the grounds.

Security logs are only valuable if analyzed effectively. Here are some key considerations...

- Log Retention: Maintain security logs for a sufficient period to facilitate investigation and compliance requirements. Imagine the palace guards archiving their patrol logs for a set timeframe to allow for future review if needed.
- Log Correlation: Utilize tools and techniques to correlate events from different logs, identifying patterns and potential threats. Imagine the palace guards comparing their patrol logs with any reports of missing treasures or suspicious activity to identify potential connections.
- Alerting: Configure alerts to notify security personnel of critical events that require immediate attention. Imagine the palace guards having a system that triggers an alarm if they detect a break-in attempt.

Implementing Security Monitoring Tools and Processes

Proactive security monitoring is paramount for safeguarding your web application from potential threats. Just as a well-fortified palace requires vigilant guards and a central command center for effective defense, so too do web applications need dedicated tools and processes to monitor for security incidents. Let's delve into some key elements that, working together, create a robust security monitoring system...

Security Information and Event Management (SIEM)

SIEM tools act as the cornerstone of security monitoring, providing a centralized view of your security landscape. Imagine a central command center within a palace, receiving and scrutinizing reports from guards stationed throughout the grounds. SIEM tools achieve this by...

- Aggregating log data from various sources within your IT infrastructure, including web applications, servers, firewalls, and network devices. This comprehensive data collection allows for a more holistic understanding of potential security issues.
- Correlating and analyzing this data to identify patterns and anomalies that might indicate suspicious activity. By correlating events from various sources, SIEM tools can detect subtle signs of an attack that individual log entries might not reveal.
- Providing real-time insights into the security posture of your application, allowing you to react swiftly to potential threats. Having a centralized dashboard with real-time data empowers security personnel to make informed decisions and prioritize security efforts based on the most critical issues.

By providing a centralized view and insightful analysis of your security data, SIEM tools empower you to make informed decisions and prioritize security efforts effectively.

Security Orchestration, Automation, and Response (SOAR)

SOAR platforms go beyond just monitoring. They introduce automation capabilities, akin to a palace equipped with a system that can automatically trigger countermeasures based on detected security breaches. SOAR platforms can significantly improve response efficiency by…

- Automating routine security tasks, such as log analysis, incident notification, and initial response procedures. This frees up valuable time for security personnel, allowing them to focus on more complex issues like investigation and remediation.
- Orchestrating responses to security incidents by automatically triggering pre-defined actions based on the severity and nature of the threat. For instance, a SOAR platform might automatically

isolate a compromised system, block malicious IP addresses, or notify security personnel of a critical breach.

By automating routine tasks and streamlining incident response, SOAR platforms empower security teams to react more efficiently and effectively to security threats. This allows them to minimize the impact of an attack and restore normalcy more quickly.

Vulnerability Scanning

Regular vulnerability scanning is crucial for proactive defense. Imagine palace guards conducting routine inspections of walls, gates, and security systems to identify any weaknesses that attackers could exploit. Vulnerability scanning tools can play a vital role in fortifying your defenses by...

- Identifying known vulnerabilities within your web application and underlying systems. These vulnerabilities could be software bugs, misconfigurations, or outdated components that attackers can exploit to gain unauthorized access or disrupt operations.
- Prioritizing vulnerabilities based on their severity and potential impact. Not all vulnerabilities are created equal. SOAR platforms can help prioritize vulnerabilities by considering factors like the exploitability of the vulnerability, the potential damage it can cause, and the ease of remediation.
- Providing guidance on remediation steps to address the identified vulnerabilities. Once a vulnerability is identified and prioritized, SOAR platforms can provide information on how to patch the vulnerability or implement workarounds to mitigate the risk.

By conducting regular vulnerability scans and taking timely action to address the identified weaknesses, you can proactively eliminate potential entry points for attackers and significantly strengthen the overall security posture of your web application.

The Synergy of Tools and Processes

It's important to remember that implementing robust security monitoring tools and processes doesn't guarantee absolute security. However, by combining these tools with well-defined security procedures and well-trained personnel, you can significantly strengthen your overall cybersecurity posture.

This multi-layered approach provides the necessary vigilance to detect, respond to, and mitigate security threats, safeguarding your web application from the ever-evolving landscape of cyberattacks. Security professionals should strive to continuously improve their security posture by staying updated on the latest threats, implementing new security measures as needed, and fostering a culture of security awareness within the organization. By following these principles, you can create a secure web application that can withstand the ever-present threats of the digital world.

Consequences of Security Logging and Monitoring Failures

In the realm of cybersecurity, organizations invest heavily in fortifying their digital perimeters with firewalls, intrusion detection systems, and access controls. However, a critical security gap often emerges — the absence of robust security logging and monitoring practices. This oversight, akin to neglecting to record guard patrols within a high-security facility, can have severe consequences for an organization's security posture. Let's explore the far-reaching ramifications of neglecting security logging and monitoring...

Delayed Detection

Without comprehensive logging and monitoring, security incidents can fester undetected for extended periods. Malicious actors, operating in the shadows, have ample time to establish a foothold within an organization's systems. Sensitive data can be exfiltrated, critical operations can be disrupted, and the extent of the damage can escalate significantly before the attack is even identified. This delayed detection mirrors a security lapse within a physical facility where guards fail to document their patrols. Unnoticed intruders can roam freely, compromising valuable assets before their presence is acknowledged.

Security logs serve as the digital equivalent of vigilant guards, constantly monitoring system activity and recording events. By analyzing these logs in real-time, security professionals can identify suspicious activity and trigger timely incident response procedures. This proactive approach significantly reduces the window of opportunity for attackers, minimizing the potential impact of a security breach.

Hindered Forensics

When a security incident comes to light, the absence of detailed logs creates a significant challenge for forensic investigations. Imagine a crime scene investigation hampered by a lack of witness reports or security footage. Similarly, without comprehensive logs, it's nearly impossible to conduct a thorough forensic analysis of a security breach. The root cause of the incident, the attacker's entry point, and the scope of the compromise remain shrouded in mystery.

Security logs provide an invaluable audit trail, documenting system activities and user actions. This granular data empowers security teams to reconstruct the timeline of an attack, identify exploited vulnerabilities, and implement targeted remediation measures. Without this crucial information, investigations become a frustrating exercise in futility, hindering the organization's ability to learn from past incidents and prevent future ones.

Regulatory Non-Compliance

The consequences of neglecting security logging and monitoring extend beyond operational inefficiencies. Many regulatory frameworks and compliance standards mandate organizations to maintain security logs for a specified period. Failure to adhere to these requirements can result in hefty fines and legal repercussions. This scenario is analogous to a physical security breach where a facility fails to maintain proper access control records, potentially incurring significant penalties from regulatory bodies.

Organizations operating in sensitive industries, such as healthcare or finance, are particularly susceptible to these regulatory ramifications. Security logging and monitoring are not just best practices; they are legal requirements. By implementing robust logging practices, organizations demonstrate their commitment to data security and regulatory compliance, safeguarding their reputation and avoiding costly legal battles.

In conclusion, neglecting security logging and monitoring creates a perilous gap in an organization's cybersecurity posture. By prioritizing these practices, organizations can equip themselves with the necessary tools to detect threats swiftly, conduct thorough investigations, and maintain compliance with industry regulations. Remember, security is an ongoing process, and robust logging and monitoring are the cornerstones of a proactive and effective security strategy.

A10: Server-Side Request Forgery (SSRF) – Exploiting Internal Resources

Imagine a magnificent palace with a highly trained messenger who can deliver any request to anyone within the castle walls. However, a mischievous trickster could exploit this system by tricking the messenger into delivering forged requests, potentially causing chaos within the palace. This scenario parallels Server-Side Request Forgery (SSRF), a vulnerability that exploits an application's ability to fetch resources from other servers.

Understanding SSRF

Imagine a grand web application, a digital castle teeming with valuable data and functionality. Lurking in the shadows are malicious actors, ever vigilant for weaknesses to exploit. One such threat is a Server-Side Request Forgery (SSRF) vulnerability, akin to a cunning trickster attempting to manipulate the castle's operations for their own gain.

SSRF - A Deceptive Forgery

An SSRF vulnerability arises when a web application processes user input and utilizes it to construct requests to external servers or resources. This functionality can be exploited by attackers who craft deceptive input, tricking the application into making unauthorized requests. Here's how it works...

- The Malicious Input: Imagine a mischievous individual, akin to a trickster, forging a letter that appears to be from a trusted source within the castle (like the king).
- The Deceived Messenger: The forged letter instructs a messenger (representing the web application) to retrieve sensitive documents stored within a restricted area of the palace (symbolizing the external server or resource).

- The Unwitting Breach: Unaware of the forgery, the messenger complies with the fabricated instructions, breaching security protocols and accessing unauthorized information.

The Perils of SSRF Attacks

In the digital realm, the consequences of SSRF attacks can be severe...

- Circumventing Access Controls: Attackers can use SSRF to bypass security measures in place, gaining access to resources that should be restricted.
- Exfiltrating Sensitive Data: By manipulating the application's requests, attackers can steal confidential information stored on internal systems.
- Exploiting Internal Systems: SSRF vulnerabilities can be leveraged to launch further attacks within the network, compromising additional systems and escalating the severity of the breach.

Defending the Web Application Castle

Understanding SSRF vulnerabilities is crucial for safeguarding web applications. Here's how developers and security professionals can fortify their defenses...

- Input Validation and Sanitization: Rigorously examine all user input to ensure it conforms to expected formats and doesn't contain malicious code. This prevents the trickster from inserting deceptive instructions within the forged letter.
- Strict Access Controls: Implement clear and well-defined access controls, limiting the application's ability to access unauthorized resources. This ensures the messenger only retrieves information from authorized locations within the palace.
- Secure Coding Practices: Adhere to secure coding principles to minimize the introduction of vulnerabilities within the application

itself. Following established security guidelines strengthens the castle walls and makes it more resistant to manipulation.

By implementing these security measures, organizations can significantly reduce the risk of SSRF attacks and safeguard their web applications from the devious plots of malicious actors. Remember, cybersecurity is an ongoing battle. Staying vigilant, understanding potential threats, and prioritizing robust security practices are essential for maintaining a secure and resilient web application castle.

Unveiling Attack Vector

Attackers can leverage SSRF vulnerabilities for various malicious purposes...

- Internal Network Exploration: Attackers can use SSRF to map the internal network of the application, identifying other servers and potential vulnerabilities. Imagine the trickster using forged requests to the messenger to inquire about the layout of the palace and the location of its various resources.
- Denial-of-Service (DoS) Attacks: Attackers can craft requests that overload internal servers, causing them to crash and disrupt operations. Imagine the trickster bombarding the messenger with forged requests, overwhelming their capacity to deliver messages, and causing chaos within the palace.
- Data Exfiltration: In certain cases, attackers might exploit SSRF to access and exfiltrate sensitive data from internal systems. Imagine the trickster using forged requests to the messenger to steal confidential documents from restricted areas within the palace.

Mitigating SSRF Risks - Protecting Trusted Messengers

Fortunately, developers can employ various techniques to mitigate the risk of SSRF attacks...

- Input Validation: Rigorously validate all user inputs to ensure they conform to expected formats and don't contain malicious URLs or protocols. Imagine the palace guards carefully inspecting any letters delivered to the messenger, verifying their authenticity, and ensuring they don't contain any hidden instructions.

- Restrict Allowed URLs: Limit the range of URLs the application can access to only those required for legitimate functionality. Imagine the messenger only being allowed to deliver messages to specific locations within the palace walls.

- Network Segmentation: Segment the internal network to restrict access between different systems. Imagine dividing the palace into separate sections with controlled access points, preventing unauthorized movement within the castle.

- Monitor for Suspicious Activity: Monitor application logs for unusual requests that might indicate SSRF attempts. Imagine the palace guards being vigilant and reporting any suspicious messages or requests delivered by the messenger.

The Importance of Context-Aware Restrictions

Within the realm of cybersecurity, access control mechanisms are paramount for safeguarding sensitive information and functionalities. These controls, akin to guards stationed at the gates of a castle, regulate who or what can access specific resources. However, implementing overly restrictive access controls can hinder legitimate operations, creating a roadblock to essential tasks. Finding the right balance is key.

Web applications often rely on the ability to access external resources to function properly. Overly restrictive access controls can inadvertently block legitimate requests for resources essential for the application's core functionalities. Context-aware restrictions allow you to create a more nuanced approach. Just as the castle guards permit messengers carrying authorized messages to pass through specific checkpoints, context-aware restrictions can grant access based on the nature of the request. This ensures that essential functionalities are not compromised while upholding security standards.

Traditionally, access control systems often operate on a binary principle: allow or deny. Imagine the castle gates being either fully open or completely shut. Context-aware restrictions introduce a more granular approach. Think of the messenger carrying a royal decree being granted access to more areas of the palace compared to a messenger bearing news from a distant village. Similarly, context-aware restrictions can define different access levels for various users or request types.

For instance, an internal user within a web application might be granted full access to internal resources, while an external user might only be allowed to access publicly available data. This tiered approach provides a more secure and adaptable environment.

Context-aware restrictions can also be dynamic, adapting to real-time situations. Imagine the castle guards raising the drawbridge and tightening security protocols during a potential siege. In the digital world, context-aware restrictions can be configured to adjust access levels based on factors like time of day, user location, or even historical behavioural patterns. This dynamic approach allows for a more responsive security posture, adapting to potential threats as they arise.

Implementing access controls is an art form. Context-aware restrictions empower you to strike the delicate balance between security and functionality. By considering the specific needs of your environment and tailoring access controls accordingly, you can create a secure and efficient system that safeguards sensitive information while allowing authorized users to perform their essential tasks. Remember, effective access control is not about creating an impenetrable fortress, but rather a secure and well-functioning environment.

OWASP - A Gateway to Security Resources

The Open Web Application Security Project (OWASP) stands as a pivotal organization within the realm of web application security. It furnishes developers, security professionals, and organizations of all sizes with a comprehensive arsenal of resources to combat cyber threats and cultivate robust web applications. This document delves into the various facets of OWASP's offerings and how they can be strategically leveraged to establish a security-centric development environment.

OWASP: Your Trusted Security Compendium

Imagine a centralized security repository dedicated to safeguarding your digital assets. OWASP embodies this trusted ally, providing a meticulously curated collection of resources encompassing best practices, methodologies, and industry-standard tools – all meticulously crafted to fortify your web application's defenses. This comprehensive compendium includes:

- **OWASP Top 10:** A continuously evolving enumeration of the ten most critical web application security risks. This benchmark serves as a cornerstone for prioritizing security efforts, enabling developers to concentrate on the vulnerabilities that pose the greatest threat.

- **Testing Guides**: In-depth guides such as the OWASP Testing Guide equip security professionals with the knowledge and methodologies to conduct effective penetration testing. These guides delve into various testing techniques, ranging from black-box testing (simulating an attacker with no prior knowledge) to gray-box testing (leveraging some knowledge about the application's internal workings).

- **Project Documentation**: Each OWASP project, such as ZAP or WAF (Web Application Firewall), offers detailed documentation to guide users in implementation and utilization. This meticulous documentation ensures that developers and security professionals can leverage these tools to their full potential.

Unveiling the Power of OWASP Projects & Tools

Envision a well-stocked security arsenal brimming with specialized tools and blueprints. OWASP boasts a diverse range of projects catering to various security needs, empowering you to select the right tools for the specific task at hand...

ZAP (Zed Attack Proxy)

ZAP, short for Zed Attack Proxy, stands as a cornerstone within the OWASP project arsenal. It's a free and open-source penetration testing tool specifically designed to empower ethical hackers and security professionals in their quest to identify vulnerabilities within web applications. Imagine wielding a versatile tool that allows you to meticulously examine and manipulate the intricate workings of a web application, akin to a security inspector thoroughly examining a building's structure and access points. Here's a deeper dive into ZAP's functionalities and how it aids in fortifying web application security:

Interception and Manipulation

ZAP functions as a powerful man-in-the-middle proxy. This enables it to intercept all communication flowing between your web browser and the target web application. Think of ZAP as a transparent bridge on the data highway, allowing you to inspect and manipulate the traffic flowing through it. ZAP empowers you to...

- View and Modify Requests: Examine the HTTP requests being sent from your browser to the application. You can modify these requests to simulate various attack scenarios, such as injecting malicious code or altering parameters to test for vulnerabilities. Imagine the security inspector being able to analyze the blueprints used to construct the building, and even modify them to assess the structural integrity under different stress conditions.

- Inspect and Modify Responses: Analyze the responses sent back by the web application to your browser. This allows you to identify potential security issues within the application's logic or configuration. You can even modify responses to test for vulnerabilities related to data manipulation or session hijacking. Imagine the security inspector being able to examine the building materials used in construction and even test their resilience against simulated attacks.

- Break Out of the Browser: ZAP isn't restricted to browser-based attacks. It allows you to craft and send raw HTTP requests, enabling you to test vulnerabilities that might not be accessible through a traditional browser interface. Imagine the security inspector not just examining the building's blueprints and access points used by occupants, but also having the ability to test the perimeter walls and security measures for vulnerabilities.

Brute Force Power with Passive and Active Scanning

ZAP offers a two-pronged approach to vulnerability detection...

- Passive Scanning: As you navigate the web application through your browser, ZAP passively scans the intercepted traffic in the background. It identifies potential vulnerabilities based on patterns and signatures within the requests and responses. Imagine the security inspector having a keen eye for identifying structural weaknesses or security lapses simply by observing how the building is used and how people move through it.

- Active Scanning: ZAP boasts a comprehensive suite of active scanners. These scanners proactively probe the web application for specific vulnerabilities. They can test for common issues like SQL injection, cross-site scripting (XSS), and insecure direct object references. Imagine the security inspector using specialized tools to meticulously examine the building's walls, doors, and security systems for any weaknesses.

Extensibility

ZAP's extensibility allows you to tailor it to your specific needs. It offers a vibrant add-on ecosystem, empowering you to expand its functionalities with extensions catering to various security testing needs. Imagine the security inspector having a modular toolkit, allowing them to add specialized tools for specific security assessments, such as lock-picking tools for testing door security or thermal scanners for identifying structural weaknesses.

Beyond the Tool - Fostering Security Awareness

ZAP isn't just a tool; it serves as a valuable training resource. Its user-friendly interface and extensive documentation make it ideal for developers and security professionals seeking to hone their penetration testing skills. Imagine the security inspector not only using advanced tools but also using their expertise to train others on building security best practices.

By leveraging ZAP's capabilities, organizations can significantly bolster the security posture of their web applications. Remember, ZAP is just one piece of the security puzzle. It should be used in conjunction with other security testing tools and methodologies for a comprehensive security assessment.

OWASP WAF (Web Application Firewall)

Fortifying your web application's security goes beyond internal testing and code reviews. A critical line of defense resides at the application's perimeter — the OWASP WAF (Web Application Firewall). Imagine a vigilant security guard stationed at the entrance of a high-security building, meticulously screening everyone who attempts entry. Similarly, the OWASP WAF acts as a watchful sentinel, scrutinizing all incoming traffic to your web application and filtering out any malicious attempts before they can reach your application server.

A Multi-Layered Defense

The OWASP WAF employs a multi-layered approach to safeguard your web application...

- Signature-Based Detection: The WAF maintains a comprehensive database of known attack signatures. It meticulously compares incoming traffic patterns to these signatures, identifying and blocking attempts that match known malicious patterns. Think of the security guard having a list of wanted criminals and checking the identification of everyone entering the building against that list.
- Anomaly Detection: Beyond just signature matching, the WAF analyzes traffic patterns for anomalies. It can identify suspicious behaviour based on factors like unusual request frequencies or unexpected data formats. Imagine the security guard not just checking IDs but also being observant of anyone acting suspiciously or attempting to enter restricted areas.
- Positive Security Model: In contrast to traditional negative security models that attempt to block everything except for explicitly allowed traffic, the OWASP WAF utilizes a positive security model. This approach defines a set of authorized actions and rigorously filters out anything that deviates from that norm.

Think of the security guard having a clear list of authorized personnel and only allowing those individuals to enter, while denying entry to anyone not on the list.

Customization for Enhanced Protection

The OWASP WAF offers a high degree of customization, enabling you to tailor its rules to your specific security needs. You can…

- Create Custom Rules: Develop your own rules to address unique threats or vulnerabilities specific to your web application. Imagine the security guard being able to adapt their screening procedures based on any specific threats or security concerns for the building.
- Block Specific IP Addresses: If you identify suspicious activity originating from specific IP addresses, you can configure the WAF to block traffic from those sources. This is akin to the security guard having the authority to deny entry to individuals on a blacklist.
- Integrate with Other Security Measures: The OWASP WAF can seamlessly integrate with other security tools and frameworks. This collaborative approach fosters a comprehensive security ecosystem for your web application. Imagine the security guard working in tandem with security cameras, alarm systems, and other security personnel to provide a robust security posture for the building.

The Advantages of Open Source

Being an open-source project, the OWASP WAF offers several advantages…

- Cost-Effectiveness: There are no licensing fees associated with deploying the OWASP WAF. This makes it an attractive solution for organizations with budget constraints. Imagine having a highly effective security guard without incurring the cost of hiring a private security firm.

- Transparency and Community Support: The open-source nature of the OWASP WAF fosters transparency and a vibrant community of developers. This translates to continuous improvement, bug fixes, and readily available support resources. Imagine the security guard benefitting from the knowledge and experience of a wider security community, staying updated on the latest threats and best practices.

- Customization and Flexibility: The open-source nature allows for extensive customization of the WAF's core functionalities. This empowers organizations to tailor the security measures to their specific web application requirements. Imagine the security guard having the flexibility to adapt their procedures based on the specific layout and security needs of the building.

By deploying the OWASP WAF as your first line of defense, you add a crucial layer of security to your web application's perimeter. This vigilant sentinel, working in conjunction with other security measures, significantly reduces the risk of malicious attacks infiltrating your web application server. Remember, security is an ongoing process. Regularly update the WAF's rules, stay informed about evolving threats, and leverage the OWASP community for continued support to ensure your web application remains a secure fortress in the digital landscape.

Optimizing Security Testing

OWASP surpasses merely providing tools; it equips you with the knowledge to wield them effectively. Resources such as the OWASP Testing Guide offer methodologies and best practices for conducting security testing throughout the entire development lifecycle. This proactive approach, outlined in resources like the OWASP Testing Guide, yields significant benefits...

- Early Detection and Resolution: By integrating security testing throughout the SDLC, vulnerabilities are identified and addressed early in the development process. This is akin to fixing cracks in a building's foundation during construction, rather than having to perform a costly and disruptive repair job later.
- Reduced Costs and Rework: Catching vulnerabilities early translates to significant cost savings. Fixing a critical flaw in the early stages of development is far less expensive than patching a deployed application that has potentially been compromised. Imagine the difference between repairing a minor leak during construction and having to replace water-damaged drywall and flooring after the building is complete.
- Improved Security Posture: By proactively testing throughout the SDLC, you cultivate a security-conscious development environment. This fosters the creation of web applications that are inherently more secure from the ground up, reducing the overall attack surface for malicious actors. Think of building a house with robust security features from the start, instead of retrofitting security measures after the house is built.

Understanding the "Why" Behind Testing Methodologies

The OWASP Testing Guide doesn't just provide a list of tools; it delves into the "why" behind various testing methodologies. Here's how this knowledge empowers security professionals...

- Targeted Testing: By understanding the strengths and limitations of different testing methodologies, security professionals can conduct more targeted testing efforts. This ensures they're focusing their resources on areas most susceptible to specific threats relevant to the application being developed. Imagine a security specialist choosing the right tools to scan for electrical wiring faults, rather than wasting time checking for plumbing leaks.

- Risk-Based Approach: The OWASP Testing Guide emphasizes a risk-based approach to security testing. This involves prioritizing testing efforts based on the likelihood and potential impact of a specific threat. Security professionals can allocate their resources towards addressing vulnerabilities that pose the greatest risk to the application, optimizing their testing efforts. Imagine a security specialist focusing on fortifying the building's main entrance and high-value storage areas, while also implementing basic security measures for less critical areas.

- Continuous Improvement: Understanding the "why" behind testing methodologies fosters a culture of continuous improvement within the development team. By analyzing test results and identifying recurring vulnerabilities, developers can refine their coding practices and security professionals can adapt their testing strategies to address evolving threats. Imagine the security team learning from past security breaches and implementing improved access control measures and security awareness training programs.

By adopting a comprehensive approach to security testing, informed by the knowledge and best practices offered by OWASP, organizations can significantly enhance the security posture of their web applications. Remember, security is an ongoing process. Continuous testing, adaptation, and learning are paramount in the ever-evolving threat landscape of the digital world.

OWASP Amass – for Attack Surface Mapping

Within the expansive toolkit curated by the Open Web Application Security Project (OWASP), Amass emerges as a potent instrument designed to illuminate the sprawling attack surfaces of modern digital ecosystems. As a cornerstone of OWASP's mission to fortify web application security, Amass empowers security practitioners and ethical hackers with the means to conduct exhaustive reconnaissance, unravelling the intricacies of organizational infrastructures and online assets.

Unveiling the Digital Landscape

At its essence, OWASP Amass serves as a digital cartographer, charting the expansive terrain of cyberspace with meticulous precision. By orchestrating comprehensive reconnaissance campaigns, this versatile tool enables users to:

- Discover Internet Assets: Amass leverages a diverse array of reconnaissance techniques to unearth a plethora of internet-facing assets associated with a target organization. From domain names and subdomains to IP addresses and network services, Amass leaves no stone unturned in its quest to delineate the digital footprint of its targets.

- Enumerate Relationships: Beyond mere asset discovery, Amass excels in elucidating the intricate relationships interwoven within the digital landscape. By unravelling the complex web of domain ownership, DNS configurations, and network interconnections, this tool provides invaluable insights into the structural fabric underpinning modern cyber infrastructures.

- Identify Vulnerabilities: Armed with a comprehensive understanding of the target's attack surface, users can discern potential vulnerabilities ripe for exploitation. Amass facilitates the identification of misconfigurations, exposed endpoints, and overlooked assets, thus empowering security practitioners to pre-emptively shore up defenses against malicious incursions.

Robust Reconnaissance Methodologies

OWASP Amass embodies OWASP's commitment to excellence in cybersecurity through its robust reconnaissance methodologies. Leveraging a blend of passive intelligence gathering, active probing, and data correlation, this tool employs a multifaceted approach to surface mapping, ensuring unparalleled depth and accuracy in its findings.

- Passive Intelligence Gathering: Amass harnesses passive reconnaissance techniques to glean insights from publicly available data sources, such as DNS records, certificate transparency logs, and internet-wide scans. By aggregating and analyzing this wealth of information, Amass unveils a comprehensive panorama of the target's digital presence.
- Active Probing: Complementing passive techniques, Amass engages in active probing to validate and augment its reconnaissance findings. Through targeted DNS queries, port scans, and service enumeration, this tool validates the existence of discovered assets and unearths additional entry points for further exploration.
- Data Correlation: By harmonizing disparate data sources and cross-referencing reconnaissance findings, Amass facilitates a holistic understanding of the target's attack surface. This process of data correlation enables users to discern meaningful patterns, identify outliers, and prioritize areas of focus for subsequent security assessments.

Empowering Security Vigilance

In alignment with OWASP's overarching mission, Amass transcends its utility as a mere tool, serving as a catalyst for fostering security vigilance and resilience. By equipping security practitioners with the means to comprehensively map and understand their organization's attack surface, Amass empowers proactive threat mitigation and risk management strategies.

Cultivating a Culture of Security Excellence

Through its user-friendly interface, extensive documentation, and active community engagement, OWASP Amass becomes more than just a tool—it becomes a cornerstone for cultivating a culture of security excellence within organizations. By imparting knowledge, sharing best practices, and fostering collaboration, Amass embodies OWASP's ethos of collective empowerment and continuous improvement in cybersecurity.

OWASP PurpleTeam

OWASP's PurpleTeam initiative emerges as a pioneering effort to harmonize the methodologies of red and blue teams within the realm of cybersecurity. By fostering collaboration, knowledge sharing, and cross-functional engagement, PurpleTeam endeavours to transcend traditional silos, enabling organizations to mount a unified defense against cyber threats.

Convergence of Red and Blue

At its core, OWASP PurpleTeam embodies the convergence of red team offensive tactics and blue team defensive strategies, culminating in a holistic approach to cybersecurity assessment and mitigation. This fusion of adversarial simulation and defensive resilience empowers organizations to...

- Simulate Real-World Threat Scenarios: PurpleTeam simulations emulate real-world cyber threats, leveraging the combined expertise of red and blue team practitioners to craft sophisticated attack scenarios. By simulating adversary tactics, techniques, and procedures (TTPs), PurpleTeam exercises enable organizations to identify and remediate vulnerabilities proactively.

- Enhance Detection and Response Capabilities: Through collaborative engagement, PurpleTeam exercises bolster organizations' detection and response capabilities, enabling blue teams to fine-tune defensive mechanisms and red teams to refine evasion and exploitation techniques. This iterative process of refinement facilitates continuous improvement in cybersecurity posture and incident readiness.
- Facilitate Knowledge Transfer and Skill Development: PurpleTeam initiatives serve as fertile ground for knowledge transfer and skill development across red and blue team disciplines. By fostering cross-training, mentorship, and information sharing, PurpleTeam endeavours to cultivate a cadre of versatile cybersecurity practitioner's adept at navigating the evolving threat landscape.

Experiential Learning and Continuous Improvement

OWASP PurpleTeam embraces a philosophy of experiential learning and continuous improvement, epitomizing OWASP's commitment to excellence in cybersecurity education and practice. Through hands-on simulations, tabletop exercises, and collaborative workshops, PurpleTeam initiatives provide practitioners with practical insights and actionable takeaways, equipping them to navigate complex cyber threats with confidence and proficiency.

Empowering Organizational Resilience

By bridging the gap between red and blue teams, OWASP PurpleTeam empowers organizations to cultivate a culture of resilience and adaptability in the face of cyber threats. Through collaborative engagement, PurpleTeam initiatives foster a shared understanding of risk, promote proactive threat mitigation strategies, and instil confidence in organizational defenses.

Community Engagement and Knowledge Sharing

In alignment with OWASP's ethos of community-driven collaboration, PurpleTeam initiatives actively engage practitioners, researchers, and industry stakeholders in knowledge sharing and best practice dissemination. Through conferences, webinars, and online forums, PurpleTeam endeavours to democratize access to cybersecurity expertise, Catalyzing innovation, and collective empowerment within the global cybersecurity community.

OWASP Dependency-Check

OWASP Dependency-Check emerges as a critical component in the arsenal of cybersecurity tools, dedicated to fortifying software supply chains against vulnerabilities lurking within dependencies. As a flagship initiative of the Open Web Application Security Project (OWASP), Dependency-Check embodies a proactive approach to risk mitigation, empowering developers, and security practitioners to identify and remediate vulnerable software components before they pose a threat.

Guarding Against Supply Chain Vulnerabilities

In an era marked by the proliferation of third-party dependencies, OWASP Dependency-Check serves as a vigilant guardian, scrutinizing software supply chains with unwavering scrutiny. By analyzing dependencies across diverse ecosystems, including libraries, frameworks, and plugins, Dependency-Check enables organizations to...

- Detect Vulnerabilities: Leveraging an extensive database of Common Vulnerabilities and Exposures (CVEs) and other security advisories, Dependency-Check systematically scans software dependencies for known vulnerabilities. Through automated analysis and pattern recognition, this tool identifies potential security risks, ranging from outdated libraries to exposed APIs.

- Assess Severity and Impact: Beyond mere detection, Dependency-Check provides valuable insights into the severity and impact of identified vulnerabilities. By contextualizing findings within the broader risk landscape, this tool empowers organizations to prioritize remediation efforts, focusing on vulnerabilities with the greatest potential for exploitation or harm.

- Facilitate Remediation: Armed with actionable intelligence, developers can swiftly remediate vulnerabilities within software dependencies. Dependency-Check integrates seamlessly into existing development workflows, providing actionable recommendations and guidance for mitigating risks through library updates, patches, or alternative solutions.

Integration and Automation

OWASP Dependency-Check embodies OWASP's commitment to automation and integration, seamlessly integrating into modern software development pipelines. By incorporating Dependency-Check into Continuous Integration (CI) and Continuous Deployment (CD) workflows, organizations can...

- Automate Vulnerability Assessment: Dependency-Check automates the vulnerability assessment process, enabling organizations to proactively identify and address security risks throughout the software development lifecycle. By embedding security checks into automated build and deployment processes, organizations can mitigate risks in real-time, minimizing exposure to potential threats.

- Ensure Compliance and Governance: Dependency-Check facilitates compliance with regulatory requirements and industry best practices by providing comprehensive visibility into software supply chain risks. By demonstrating due diligence in vulnerability management, organizations can enhance trust and credibility with customers, partners, and regulatory authorities.

Empowering Secure Development Practices

In alignment with OWASP's mission to advance secure development practices, Dependency-Check fosters a culture of proactive risk management and accountability within development teams. By empowering developers with the tools and knowledge to identify and remediate vulnerabilities early in the development lifecycle, Dependency-Check enables organizations to build resilient, secure software products that inspire confidence and trust.

Community-Driven Collaboration

As a cornerstone of the OWASP ecosystem, Dependency-Check embodies the principles of community-driven collaboration and knowledge sharing. Through active engagement with developers, security researchers, and industry stakeholders, Dependency-Check evolves in response to emerging threats and evolving best practices, ensuring its relevance and effectiveness in safeguarding software supply chains.

CodeSec – Scan

Within its expansive repertoire of tools and resources, CodeSec - Scan emerges as a quintessential instrument tailored to fortify web application defenses. As an OWASP-sponsored initiative, CodeSec - Scan embodies the organization's commitment to fostering security excellence across digital domains.

Empowering Security Vigilance

CodeSec - Scan embodies OWASP's ethos of empowering security vigilance within digital ecosystems. Crafted with meticulous attention to detail, this tool serves as a linchpin in the arsenal of ethical hackers, security professionals, and developers alike. By facilitating comprehensive vulnerability assessments, CodeSec - Scan equips stakeholders with the insights necessary to pre-emptively thwart malicious incursions.

Interception and Manipulation: Unveiling Vulnerabilities

At its core, CodeSec - Scan mirrors the functionality of a seasoned security inspector, adept at uncovering vulnerabilities lurking beneath the surface of web applications. Through its prowess in interception and manipulation, this tool enables users to:

- Inspect and Modify Requests: Dive deep into the labyrinth of HTTP requests coursing between browsers and target applications. By scrutinizing and modifying these requests, users can simulate diverse attack scenarios, ranging from code injections to parameter alterations, thus illuminating potential security weaknesses.
- Analyze and Manipulate Responses: Delve into the responses emanating from the target application, dissecting them with surgical precision. By identifying anomalies and potential vulnerabilities within these responses, users can gauge the resilience of the application's logic and configuration against adversarial exploits.
- Expand Beyond Browser Confines: CodeSec - Scan transcends conventional browser-centric assessments, empowering users to craft and dispatch raw HTTP requests. This capability enables the exploration of vulnerabilities that may elude traditional testing methodologies, thereby bolstering the comprehensiveness of security assessments.

Synergistic Scanning Strategies

CodeSec - Scan embodies a two-pronged approach to vulnerability detection, reminiscent of OWASP's holistic security paradigm.

- Passive Scanning: As users navigate through web applications, CodeSec- Scan diligently conducts passive scans on intercepted traffic. Leveraging pattern recognition and signature analysis, this mode of scanning unveils latent vulnerabilities, akin to a vigilant security inspector discerning structural weaknesses through observant scrutiny.

- Active Scanning: Bolstered by a suite of active scanners, CodeSec-Scan proactively probes target applications for specific vulnerabilities. Armed with specialized algorithms, these scanners meticulously scrutinize common pitfalls such as SQL injection and cross-site scripting, echoing OWASP's commitment to proactive threat mitigation.

Adaptability and Extensibility

In alignment with OWASP's ethos of inclusivity and innovation, CodeSec - Scan boasts unparalleled adaptability and extensibility. Its vibrant ecosystem of add-ons empowers users to tailor the tool to their unique security testing needs. This modular approach facilitates the integration of specialized tools and techniques, enriching the depth and breadth of vulnerability assessments.

Cultivating Security Awareness

Beyond its utility as a mere tool, CodeSec - Scan serves as a catalyst for cultivating security awareness and expertise. With its user-friendly interface and comprehensive documentation, this OWASP-sponsored initiative becomes an invaluable resource for developers, security professionals, and aspiring enthusiasts alike. By imparting knowledge and fostering best practices, CodeSec - Scan embodies OWASP's commitment to nurturing a culture of security excellence.

In essence, CodeSec - Scan epitomizes OWASP's unwavering dedication to advancing cybersecurity principles and practices. As organizations embrace this tool within their security arsenal, they embark on a journey towards fortified defenses and heightened resilience in the face of evolving threats.

OWASP DefectDojo

OWASP DefectDojo emerges as a cornerstone in the realm of vulnerability management, providing organizations with a robust platform to streamline the identification, tracking, and remediation of security vulnerabilities. As an initiative of the Open Web Application Security Project (OWASP), DefectDojo embodies a proactive approach to cybersecurity, empowering teams to collaboratively address vulnerabilities and fortify their defenses against evolving threats.

Centralized Vulnerability Tracking

At its core, OWASP DefectDojo serves as a centralized hub for vulnerability tracking, aggregating data from diverse sources and providing stakeholders with comprehensive visibility into the organization's security posture. Key functionalities include...

- Vulnerability Import: DefectDojo enables the import of vulnerability data from various scanners, including static analysis tools, dynamic scanners, and manual assessments. By consolidating findings into a unified repository, DefectDojo facilitates centralized management and analysis of vulnerabilities across the organization's software assets.

- Risk Prioritization: Leveraging a robust risk scoring framework, DefectDojo facilitates the prioritization of vulnerabilities based on severity, impact, and likelihood of exploitation. By providing actionable insights into the most critical security risks, DefectDojo empowers teams to allocate resources effectively and focus remediation efforts where they are needed most.

- Collaborative Workflow: DefectDojo fosters collaboration among cross-functional teams involved in vulnerability management, including developers, security analysts, and project managers. Through customizable workflows, task assignments, and notifications, DefectDojo streamlines the remediation process, ensuring timely resolution of security issues.

Customizable Reporting and Analytics

OWASP DefectDojo equips organizations with powerful reporting and analytics capabilities, enabling stakeholders to derive actionable insights from vulnerability data and track progress over time. Key features include:

- Customizable Reports: DefectDojo offers a range of pre-configured reports and dashboards, as well as the flexibility to create custom reports tailored to specific requirements. By visualizing vulnerability trends, remediation status, and compliance metrics, DefectDojo empowers stakeholders to make informed decisions and communicate effectively with key stakeholders.
- Trend Analysis: DefectDojo enables organizations to track vulnerability trends over time, identifying recurring issues, emerging threats, and areas of improvement. By analyzing historical data and benchmarking against industry standards, DefectDojo facilitates continuous improvement in vulnerability management practices and informs strategic decision-making.
- Compliance Monitoring: DefectDojo supports compliance monitoring and reporting requirements by providing visibility into security vulnerabilities and their impact on regulatory and contractual obligations. By generating compliance reports and audit trails, DefectDojo helps organizations demonstrate due diligence and maintain alignment with legal and industry standards.

Open and Extensible Platform

In alignment with OWASP's commitment to open-source principles and community-driven collaboration, DefectDojo is an open and extensible platform that encourages contributions from developers, security researchers, and industry practitioners.

- Modular Architecture: DefectDojo's modular architecture allows for easy integration with third-party tools and services, enabling organizations to extend its functionality and adapt it to their unique requirements. By leveraging a vibrant ecosystem of plugins and extensions, DefectDojo evolves in response to emerging threats and evolving best practices.
- Active Community Engagement: DefectDojo benefits from active community engagement, with a dedicated community of users and contributors who share knowledge, collaborate on development, and provide support to fellow practitioners. Through forums, mailing lists, and community events, DefectDojo fosters a culture of knowledge sharing and collective empowerment.

OWASP Cheat Sheets

OWASP Cheat Sheets are a vital component within the security arsenal, offering developers readily accessible knowledge nuggets to fortify their coding practices. Imagine a soldier on the battlefield equipped with a reference card outlining combat tactics and enemy weaknesses. Similarly, OWASP Cheat Sheets empower developers with critical security information at their fingertips. These concise and downloadable resources encompass a vast array of security topics, including...

- Secure Coding Practices: Cheat sheets provide a quick reference guide for secure coding principles. This can include guidance on input validation, proper data storage techniques, and error handling practices – all essential for building applications resilient against common attacks.
- Specific Vulnerabilities: Certain cheat sheets delve into specific web application security vulnerabilities like SQL injection or Cross-

Site Scripting (XSS). These resources outline the nature of the vulnerability, potential mitigation strategies, and code examples to illustrate secure coding practices.

- Testing Methodologies: Some cheat sheets provide a brief overview of testing methodologies like black-box or white-box testing. This equips developers with a basic understanding of how their code might be evaluated, allowing them to write code that is more conducive to security testing.

Benefits of OWASP Cheat Sheets

- Accessibility: The downloadable format allows developers to readily access these resources, whether working online or offline.
- Quick Reference: The concise nature of the cheat sheets makes them ideal for quick consultations during coding sessions or code reviews. Developers can swiftly refresh their memory on secure coding practices or gain insights into specific vulnerabilities.
- Improved Code Quality: By having security best practices readily available, developers are empowered to write more secure code from the outset. This reduces the likelihood of vulnerabilities being introduced during development, saving time and resources in the long run.
- Enhanced Collaboration: OWASP Cheat Sheets provide a common frame of reference for developers and security professionals. This fosters a collaborative environment where security concerns can be effectively communicated and addressed during the development process.

Utilizing Cheat Sheets Effectively

Here are some tips to maximize the effectiveness of OWASP Cheat Sheets within your development workflow...

- Integrate into Development Process: Distribute cheat sheets to developers and encourage them to reference them during coding sessions and code reviews.
- Conduct Training Sessions: Consider conducting training sessions specifically focused on OWASP Cheat Sheets. This can help developers understand the content and how to apply it effectively in their daily work.
- Promote Continuous Learning: Security is an ever-evolving landscape. Encourage developers to stay updated with the latest OWASP Cheat Sheets as new resources are released or existing ones are revised.

By strategically incorporating OWASP Cheat Sheets into your development environment, you can empower your developers to become active participants in the security process. This fosters a culture of security awareness and ultimately leads to the creation of more robust and secure web applications. Remember, security is a shared responsibility, and developers play a crucial role in safeguarding your applications against evolving cyber threats.

OWASP Juice Shop - for Secure Coding Education

OWASP Juice Shop represents a groundbreaking initiative within the cybersecurity community, offering a gamified platform for developers and security enthusiasts to hone their skills in secure coding, vulnerability assessment, and penetration testing. As an OWASP project, Juice Shop embodies the organization's commitment to advancing cybersecurity education and fostering a culture of proactive risk management.

Interactive Learning Environment

OWASP Juice Shop serves as an interactive learning environment where participants can engage in realistic scenarios to explore and address security vulnerabilities within web applications.

- Vulnerable Application: Juice Shop provides participants with access to a deliberately insecure web application, populated with a wide range of security vulnerabilities commonly found in real-world software. By interacting with the application, users can identify, exploit, and remediate vulnerabilities, gaining valuable hands-on experience in secure coding practices and penetration testing techniques.

- Gamified Challenges: Juice Shop incorporates gamification elements, including challenges, missions, and leader boards, to motivate and incentivize participation. By completing challenges and earning points, users can track their progress, compete with peers, and unlock achievements, fostering engagement and retention of learning objectives.

- Educational Resources: Juice Shop offers a wealth of educational resources, including documentation, tutorials, and walkthroughs, to support participants in their learning journey. By providing contextual guidance and explanations, Juice Shop empowers users to deepen their understanding of security concepts and apply them effectively in practice.

Real-World Application Scenarios

OWASP Juice Shop simulates real-world application scenarios, enabling participants to explore security vulnerabilities and attack vectors commonly encountered in modern web applications. Key scenarios include...

- Injection Attacks: Juice Shop exposes participants to injection vulnerabilities, such as SQL injection, NoSQL injection, and command injection, allowing them to understand the underlying principles and techniques for exploiting these vulnerabilities.

- Cross-Site Scripting (XSS): Juice Shop demonstrates various types of cross-site scripting vulnerabilities, including reflected XSS, stored XSS, and DOM-based XSS, illustrating the potential impact on user data and application functionality.
- Broken Authentication: Juice Shop highlights common authentication and session management flaws, such as weak passwords, session fixation, and insecure password recovery mechanisms, emphasizing the importance of robust authentication controls.

Community Engagement and Collaboration

As an open-source project, OWASP Juice Shop thrives on community engagement and collaboration, welcoming contributions from developers, security researchers, and educators worldwide.

- Active Development: Juice Shop benefits from active development and ongoing enhancements, with regular updates and releases incorporating new features, improvements, and security fixes. By leveraging community feedback and contributions, Juice Shop evolves in response to emerging threats and evolving best practices.
- Community Support: Juice Shop fosters a supportive community of users and contributors, who share knowledge, collaborate on development, and provide assistance to fellow participants. Through forums, mailing lists, and community events, Juice Shop cultivates a culture of learning and knowledge sharing within the cybersecurity community.

OWASP Juice Shop thus stands as a pioneering initiative in cybersecurity education, offering a dynamic platform for hands-on learning and skills development in secure coding and penetration testing. By providing participants with a realistic and engaging environment to explore security vulnerabilities and best practices, Juice Shop empowers individuals and organizations to enhance their cybersecurity capabilities and build more resilient software applications.

OWASP and the Secure Development Lifecycle (SDL)

Security shouldn't be an afterthought; it necessitates integration into the fabric of the development process from the very beginning. OWASP provides invaluable guidance on implementing a Secure Development Lifecycle (SDL) – a structured approach that integrates security considerations throughout all stages of development. Imagine the security arsenal offering not just tools and knowledge but also a comprehensive blueprint for constructing a secure fortress. By adhering to the SDL guidelines and leveraging OWASP resources, organizations can cultivate a development environment that prioritizes security from the initial planning stages to deployment and maintenance. This fosters the creation of inherently secure web applications that are less susceptible to cyberattacks.

Empowering Your Development Workforce

Having explored the various resources and tools offered by OWASP, let's delve into how organizations can leverage these offerings to cultivate a culture of security awareness within their development teams. This cultural shift is fundamental to building a robust security posture and fostering the creation of web applications that are inherently more resilient against cyber threats.

Fostering Security Champions

Imagine having security advocates embedded within the development teams themselves. OWASP's resources can be instrumental in identifying and empowering security champions within your development workforce. These individuals can...

- Champion secure coding practices: Security champions can act as internal advocates for secure coding practices, promoting the use of OWASP resources like the Top 10 list and cheat sheets during code reviews and development discussions.

- Bridge the communication gap: Security champions can bridge the communication gap between developers and security professionals. They can translate complex security concepts into actionable steps for developers and help to alleviate any apprehension developers might have towards security processes.

- Stay up-to-date on security trends: Security champions can actively stay up-to-date on the latest security trends and vulnerabilities. By leveraging OWASP resources like project documentation and community forums, they can stay informed and share this knowledge with their development teams.

Integrating Security Training

Security awareness doesn't happen overnight; it requires ongoing education and training. Here's how OWASP resources can be integrated into a comprehensive security training program...

- OWASP Top 10 as a Training Foundation: The OWASP Top 10 list serves as a valuable training foundation, providing developers with a clear understanding of the most critical web application security risks. Training modules can be built around each of the top 10 vulnerabilities, outlining mitigation strategies and best practices.

- OWASP Testing Guide for Advanced Learners: For developers seeking to delve deeper into security testing methodologies, the OWASP Testing Guide provides a comprehensive resource. Training sessions based on this guide can equip developers with the knowledge and skills to conduct basic security testing activities, enhancing their ability to identify and address vulnerabilities within their code.

- OWASP Project-Specific Training: Many OWASP projects, such as ZAP, offer dedicated training materials and workshops. These resources can be leveraged to provide developers with hands-on experience using specific security tools, empowering them to integrate these tools effectively into their development workflows.

Building a Security-Conscious Development Environment

Imagine a development environment where security is not just a consideration, but a core principle. Here's how OWASP helps foster this environment:

- Integrating Security Testing Tools: OWASP projects like ZAP can be seamlessly integrated into the development pipeline. This allows for automated security scans to be conducted throughout the development cycle, identifying potential vulnerabilities early on and allowing developers to address them promptly.
- Promoting Open Communication: OWASP resources encourage open communication and collaboration between developers and security professionals. This fosters a culture of shared responsibility for security, ensuring that security concerns are addressed proactively throughout the development process.
- Celebrating Security Wins: Recognizing and celebrating security wins within the development team can go a long way in boosting morale and further emphasizing the importance of security. Identifying and acknowledging developers who consistently adhere to secure coding practices or actively participate in security testing activities can create a positive reinforcement loop, encouraging continued security focus.

By strategically leveraging OWASP resources and fostering a culture of security awareness, organizations can empower their development teams to create secure web applications that can withstand the ever-evolving

Advanced Techniques for Web Application Security

We've explored the foundational concepts of secure design principles and testing methodologies. Now, let's delve deeper into specific strategies to fortify your web application's security...

Threat Modelling for Web Applications

Identifying Your Assets

The first step is understanding what you're protecting. This involves creating an inventory of critical assets within your application. This could include user data (login credentials, personal information), financial information (payment details), intellectual property (source code, proprietary data), and application functionality itself (availability, integrity). Imagine a security consultant meticulously examining a bank's security measures, identifying not just the vault (critical data) but also the security of cash registers (transactional data) and access control systems (application functionality).

Threat Landscape Exploration

With your assets identified, delve into potential threats. Frameworks like STRIDE (Spoofing, Tampering, Repudiation, Information Disclosure, Denial-of-Service, Elevation of Privilege) provide a structured approach for brainstorming these threats. Imagine the security consultant considering various attack scenarios, from social engineering attempts to gain unauthorized access (Spoofing) to exploiting vulnerabilities in the login system to steal passwords (Information Disclosure).

Prioritization and Mitigation

Not all threats are created equal. Analyze the likelihood and potential impact of each threat to prioritize your security efforts. Develop mitigation strategies to address the most critical threats. This might involve implementing strong authentication mechanisms, input validation to prevent malicious code injection, and encryption for sensitive data at rest and in transit. Think of the security consultant prioritizing fortifying the vault door (against high-impact theft attempts) while also installing security cameras and alarms throughout the bank (against broader security concerns).

Secure Coding Practices for Developers

Defense in Depth

Secure coding practices are the building blocks of a secure application. Developers should adhere to secure coding principles throughout the development process. This includes practices like:

- Input validation: Sanitizing user inputs to prevent injection attacks like SQL injection or XSS.
- Secure data storage: Encrypting sensitive data at rest and in transit.
- Proper error handling: Avoiding revealing sensitive information through error messages.
- Using secure libraries and frameworks: Utilizing well-maintained components with a strong security track record.

Imagine construction workers following safety guidelines while building a house – using the right materials, adhering to structural integrity principles, and implementing proper safety measures during construction. Secure coding practices are analogous to these safety measures, ensuring the application's foundation is secure from the ground up.

Staying Up-to-Date

The security landscape is constantly evolving. Developers should stay updated on the latest security vulnerabilities and coding best practices.

Resources like OWASP Top 10 (Open Web Application Security Project) provide valuable guidance for developers to stay ahead of the curve. Imagine construction workers attending safety seminars and receiving updates on new building codes and safety regulations.

Web Application Penetration Testing with OWASP Tools

Simulating Real-World Attacks

Penetration testing (pen testing) is a crucial aspect of web application security. It involves ethical hackers simulating real-world attacks to identify exploitable weaknesses in the application's defenses. OWASP (Open Web Application Security Project) provides a vast arsenal of free and open-source tools to empower security professionals to conduct pen testing effectively.

Tools for the Trade

Tools like ZAP (Zed Attack Proxy) and Burp Suite are popular choices for pen testers. These tools allow them to intercept and manipulate traffic between the application and the user, mimicking attacker techniques to probe for vulnerabilities. Imagine the ethical hackers using specialized tools to analyze the bank's security system, attempting to bypass security measures and identify weaknesses.

Beyond Automation

While automated tools play a vital role, pen testing is ultimately a human-driven process. Skilled pen testers can leverage their expertise and creativity to uncover vulnerabilities that might evade automated scanners. Think of the ethical hackers not just using tools to scan the bank's security system, but also attempting social engineering tactics on guards or exploiting less obvious weaknesses in the physical security measures.

Integrating OWASP into Agile Development Methodologies

Security as a Continuous Thread

 OWASP isn't just a collection of tools; it's a philosophy that emphasizes integrating security throughout the development lifecycle. This aligns perfectly with Agile methodologies that promote iterative development and continuous improvement.

Communication and Collaboration

Building a security-conscious development team requires fostering open communication and collaboration between developers, security professionals, and other stakeholders. OWASP resources provide a common language and framework for discussing security concerns. Imagine the security consultant working closely with the architects, construction workers, and bank managers throughout the building process. This collaboration ensures everyone is aware of security risks and works together to implement effective mitigation strategies.

Security Champions

Agile teams can benefit from designating security champions. These individuals act as advocates for secure coding practices and serve as a point of contact for security-related questions within the development team. Think of a security-focused project manager within the bank's construction team, ensuring best practices are followed and liaising with the security consultant for any arising concerns.

Automated Security Testing

While manual pen testing remains invaluable, Agile methodologies favour automation wherever possible. OWASP ZAP can be integrated into the development pipeline to perform automated security scans throughout the development cycle. Imagine security cameras and alarms being integrated into the bank's security system, providing constant monitoring and alerting for suspicious activity.

By embracing these strategies and integrating OWASP's philosophy into Agile development, organizations can create a culture of security awareness within their development teams. This continuous focus on security throughout the development lifecycle fosters the creation of web applications that are not only functionally sound but also inherently more secure and resilient against the ever-present threats of the digital landscape. Remember, security is an ongoing journey, not a destination. By consistently evaluating, testing, and refining your security practices, you can ensure your web applications remain a fortress against evolving cyber threats.

Appendix 1 - Testing Checklist - Web Application Security

The OWASP Web Application Security Testing Checklist you provided offers a comprehensive breakdown of various steps involved in securing web applications. Let's delve deeper into each section and explore its significance...

Information Gathering

Information gathering is the foundation of any successful security assessment. It involves meticulously collecting information about the web application, its functionalities, underlying technologies, and potential attack surfaces. This knowledge empowers testers to tailor their testing approach and identify vulnerabilities that could be exploited by attackers. Here's a breakdown of the various techniques employed during information gathering...

Manual Exploration

- Testers act as curious users: They manually browse the application, interacting with menus, forms, and functionalities to understand its intended behaviour. This helps identify areas that might be susceptible to user input manipulation or exploitation.
- Identifying attack surfaces: Manual exploration reveals potential entry points for attackers, such as login forms, file upload sections, or search functionalities.

Automated Techniques

- Spidering and Crawling: Automated tools can systematically crawl through the application, discovering all accessible URLs, directories, and hidden content. This helps uncover areas that might be missed during manual exploration.

File Analysis

- Scrutinizing configuration files: Files like robots.txt and sitemap.xml can provide valuable information about the application's structure and content. Analyzing these files might reveal unintended directory listings or sensitive information leaks.
- Hunting for hidden files: Certain operating systems create hidden files that might contain sensitive data. Tools can be used to identify and analyze these files, but caution is advised to avoid modifying critical system files.

External Sources

- Search Engine Cache: Sometimes, search engines cache older versions of webpages that might contain information not present on the live website. Analyzing this cached content can reveal vulnerabilities that have since been patched.
- User-Agent Analysis: Web applications might serve different content based on the User-Agent header sent by the client (browser, mobile app). Analyzing these variations can expose vulnerabilities specific to certain client types.

Technical Analysis

- Web Application Fingerprinting: Tools can identify the underlying technologies, frameworks, and libraries used to build the application. This knowledge helps testers leverage known vulnerabilities associated with those specific technologies.

Mapping the Attack Surface

- Identifying all hosts and ports: A comprehensive understanding of all servers, applications, and network ports involved in the application's operation is crucial. This helps ensure no potential entry points are overlooked.

- Related applications: Web applications often interact with other applications on the same network. Identifying these dependencies helps assess potential security risks that might arise from those interactions.

By employing these information gathering techniques, testers gain a comprehensive understanding of the application's landscape. This knowledge empowers them to conduct more targeted and effective security testing, ultimately leading to a more secure web application. Remember, information gathering is an iterative process. As new information is discovered, it can inform and refine the testing approach throughout the assessment.

Configuration Management

Configuration management plays a vital role in web application security. Improper configuration can expose vulnerabilities that attackers can exploit to gain unauthorized access, steal sensitive data, or disrupt application functionality. Here's a closer look at the areas testers focus on within configuration management...

URL and File Analysis

- Discovery: Identify commonly used application management URLs that might not be intended for public access. These URLs could potentially be used for administrative tasks or accessing sensitive information. Tools can be used to automate URL discovery and identify potential vulnerabilities.
- Unused or Outdated Files: Look for unused files or directories within the application's file structure. These files might contain outdated code, sensitive information, or backdoor scripts left behind by developers. Removing unused files reduces the attack surface and potential security risks.

HTTP Methods and Tracing

- Supported Methods: Verify that the application only allows and processes HTTP methods (GET, POST, PUT, DELETE, etc.) that are necessary for its intended functionality. Disabling unused methods helps prevent exploitation attempts that rely on unsupported functionalities.
- Cross-Site Tracing (XST): Attackers might manipulate HTTP headers to leak sensitive information from the application. Testers explore potential XST vulnerabilities by crafting malicious requests that exploit weaknesses in how the application handles headers.

Security Headers and Policies

- Content Security Policy (CSP): This security header restricts where the application can load resources from (scripts, stylesheets, images). Testing verifies that a CSP is implemented and configured appropriately to prevent loading malicious content from unauthorized sources.
- Clickjacking Protection: Clickjacking attacks involve tricking users into clicking on hidden elements on a webpage. The X-Frame-Options header can be used to prevent the application from being loaded within a frame of another website, mitigating clickjacking risks. Testing verifies the presence and effectiveness of this header.
- HSTS (HTTP Strict Transport Security): As mentioned earlier, HSTS enforces secure connections (HTTPS) for all communication with the application. Testing ensures HSTS is properly configured to prevent accidental connections over insecure HTTP.

Sensitive Data Handling

- Client-Side Code: Sensitive information like API keys or database credentials should never be embedded directly in client-side code

(JavaScript) as it can be easily extracted by attackers. Testing focuses on identifying and mitigating such practices.

- Non-Production Data: Ensure that data used in development or testing environments (e.g., development databases) is not inadvertently exposed in the live production environment. This can happen due to misconfigured access controls or accidental data leaks. Testing verifies that proper data handling practices are followed throughout the application lifecycle.
- URL and File Analysis: Checking for commonly used application management URLs and exploring for unused or outdated files can reveal vulnerabilities that attackers might exploit to gain unauthorized access or control.

Secure Transmission

When it comes to web application security, ensuring secure transmission of data between users and the application is paramount. This is where SSL/TLS (Secure Sockets Layer/Transport Layer Security) comes into play. The OWASP checklist emphasizes evaluating the SSL/TLS configuration to guarantee sensitive information like passwords, credit card details, and other confidential data remains protected during transmission. Here's a breakdown of what to look for during SSL/TLS configuration assessment...

- TLS Version: The application should use the latest and most secure version of TLS possible. Older versions (like SSLv3 and TLS 1.0) are known to have vulnerabilities and should be disabled.
- Encryption Algorithms: The chosen encryption algorithms for both key exchange and data encryption should be robust and industry-standard. Strong cipher suites like those using AES (Advanced Encryption Standard) with at least 128-bit keys are recommended.
- Key Length: The length of the encryption key directly impacts the difficulty of cracking the encryption. Testing verifies that the application uses keys with sufficient length (ideally 2048 bits or higher for RSA keys) to provide adequate security.

- Certificate Validity: The SSL/TLS certificate installed on the server needs to be valid and issued by a trusted Certificate Authority (CA). Testing ensures the certificate is not expired, revoked, or issued for a domain name mismatch.

Additional Considerations

- Perfect Forward Secrecy (PFS): This security feature ensures that even if an attacker compromises the server's private key, they cannot decrypt past captured traffic. Testing verifies that the chosen ciphersuites support PFS.
- HTTP Strict Transport Security (HSTS): This security header instructs web browsers to only connect to the application using HTTPS, enforcing secure connections. Testing verifies that HSTS is properly configured.
- SSL/TLS Configuration: Evaluating the SSL/TLS configuration for its version, encryption algorithms, key length, and certificate validity ensures that data is transmitted securely between the application and the user.

Authentication and Session Management

Authentication and session management are fundamental pillars of web application security. They work together to ensure only authorized users can access the application and maintain secure sessions once logged in. Let's delve deeper into the testing approaches for each of these areas...

Authentication Security

- User Enumeration: Attackers might try to identify existing usernames through various techniques. Testing focuses on identifying and mitigating weaknesses that could reveal usernames, such as error messages or predictable user ID sequences.

- Bypassing Authentication Mechanisms: Applications often employ mechanisms like login forms or multi-factor authentication (MFA). Testers attempt to bypass these mechanisms by exploiting vulnerabilities in the implementation. This might involve manipulating session cookies, password reset functionalities, or weaknesses in social login integrations.
- Brute-Force Attacks: These attacks involve systematically trying different username and password combinations to gain unauthorized access. Testing assesses the application's resilience against brute-force attacks by verifying:
- Rate Limiting: Limiting the number of login attempts allowed within a timeframe to discourage brute-force attempts.
- Account Lockout: Locking accounts after exceeding a certain number of failed login attempts to prevent persistent attacks.
- Strong Password Requirements: Enforcing complex password policies with minimum length, character diversity, and disallowing easily guessable combinations.

Session Management Security

- Session Token Security: Sessions are often identified by unique tokens assigned to users after successful login. Testing focuses on ensuring these tokens are:
- Cryptographically Secure: Generated using strong random values to prevent prediction or brute-forcing.
- Unique Per User: Issued uniquely to each user to prevent session hijacking (taking over another user's session).
- Limited Lifetime: Set to expire after a period of inactivity to minimize the risk of unauthorized access even if a token is compromised.
- HTTPS Enforcement: All communication between the application and user should happen over HTTPS to encrypt session data (including tokens) during transmission. This prevents attackers from eavesdropping and stealing sensitive information.

- Session Termination: Sessions should be terminated properly when users log out or after a period of inactivity. Testing verifies that session tokens are invalidated upon logout, and mechanisms are in place to prevent session fixation (reusing a valid token from a previous session).

Additional Considerations

- Two-Factor Authentication (MFA): Implementing MFA adds an extra layer of security by requiring a second verification factor (e.g., code from a mobile app) in addition to a password. Testing ensures MFA is functioning correctly and provides a robust defense against unauthorized access attempts.
- Secure Password Storage: Passwords should never be stored in plain text. Testing verifies that the application uses strong hashing algorithms (e.g., bcrypt) to store passwords securely.

Authentication Security: Testing for vulnerabilities related to user accounts, such as user enumeration (discovering existing usernames), bypassing authentication mechanisms, brute-force attacks, and weak password policies helps strengthen the login process.

- Session Management Security: Assessing how the application handles user sessions is critical. Testing focuses on session token security (avoiding predictable or guessable tokens), enforcing HTTPS for all session activity, and ensuring proper session termination to prevent unauthorized access even after successful login.

Authorization

Within the realm of web application security, access control testing plays a critical role. It verifies that the application enforces proper access control mechanisms, ensuring users can only access the resources and functionalities they are authorized for. Here's a breakdown of key areas testers focus on...

Vulnerability Hunting

- Path Traversal: Attackers might exploit vulnerabilities in how the application handles file paths to access unauthorized directories or files. Testers attempt to manipulate paths to navigate outside intended areas and access restricted resources.
- Schema Bypassing: Applications often interact with databases using a schema (structure) to define data access. Weaknesses in schema validation can allow attackers to bypass intended access controls and retrieve unauthorized data. Testers look for ways to manipulate queries to access data beyond their permitted scope.
- Vertical Privilege Escalation: This occurs when a user with low privileges manages to gain access to functionalities or data reserved for users with higher privileges (e.g., an editor gaining access to administrative functions). Testers attempt to exploit weaknesses in the application's permission checks to elevate their privileges.
- Horizontal Privilege Escalation: This happens when a user can access resources or data belonging to other users with the same privilege level. Testers try to manipulate the application to access data or functionalities associated with other user accounts.

Testing Techniques

- Black-Box Testing: Simulates an attacker's perspective by testing the application without prior knowledge of its internal workings. Testers try various techniques to exploit potential access control vulnerabilities.
- Gray-Box Testing: Combines elements of black-box and white-box testing. Testers have some knowledge of the application's

architecture but focus on finding vulnerabilities from an attacker's standpoint.

- Fuzzing: Automated tools can be used to feed the application with unexpected or malformed data to identify weaknesses in access control mechanisms.

Strengthening Access Control

- Principle of Least Privilege: Grant users the minimum level of access necessary to perform their tasks. This reduces the potential damage if a user's account gets compromised.
- Role-Based Access Control (RBAC): Define user roles with specific permissions and assign users to appropriate roles. This simplifies access management and reduces the risk of accidental misconfigurations.
- Regular Reviews and Audits: Periodically review access control policies and conduct penetration testing to identify and address any emerging vulnerabilities.

Data Validation

Input validation testing is a fundamental pillar of web application security. It involves meticulously examining all user input to ensure it conforms to expected formats and doesn't harbour malicious code. Here's a deeper dive into why it's crucial and how it's conducted...

Why is Input Validation Testing Important?

- Injection Attacks: Attackers can exploit weaknesses in data validation to inject malicious code (like SQL queries, scripts) into user input. This code can then be executed by the application, potentially leading to data breaches, unauthorized access, or even complete system compromise. Common injection attacks include

SQL injection (targeting databases), XSS (exploiting scripts in web pages), and LDAP injection (targeting directory services).

- Data Manipulation: Improper validation can allow attackers to manipulate data submitted through forms or other user interactions. This could involve altering data to gain unauthorized access, disrupt application functionality, or steal sensitive information.

How is Input Validation Testing Conducted?

- Identifying Input Points: The first step involves identifying all points where users can provide input, such as login forms, search bars, registration pages, and comment sections.
- Defining Validation Rules: For each input point, define clear validation rules that specify the allowed data format, length, characters, and range (e.g., numbers only, email address format).
- Testing with Diverse Inputs: Design test cases that encompass a wide range of valid and invalid inputs, including special characters, unexpected data types, and potential injection attempts. Here are some common techniques:
- Boundary Testing: Testing with values at the edge of allowed ranges (e.g., minimum and maximum lengths for text fields).
- Equivalence Partitioning: Dividing valid and invalid inputs into categories and testing representative data from each category.
- Injection Attacks: Crafting test cases that attempt to inject malicious code for various injection vulnerabilities (SQL injection, XSS, etc.).

Best Practices for Input Validation

- Server-Side Validation: Never rely solely on client-side validation (using JavaScript in the browser). Always implement robust validation on the server-side to ensure malicious input gets filtered out before it can cause harm.

- Input Sanitization: Even after validation, it's recommended to sanitize user input by removing or encoding potentially harmful characters. This adds an extra layer of security.
- Error Handling: Provide informative error messages when invalid input is detected. These messages should guide users towards providing correct data without revealing sensitive information about the application's vulnerabilities.
- Input Validation Testing: This is crucial to prevent injection attacks (SQL injection, Cross-Site Scripting (XSS), LDAP injection, etc.) where malicious code is injected as user input and executed by the application. Testers also look for other data validation issues that might allow attackers to manipulate data or compromise the application.

Denial-of-Service (DoS) Prevention

Denial-of-Service (DoS) attacks aim to overwhelm an application or server with excessive traffic, rendering it unavailable to legitimate users. DoS testing plays a crucial role in identifying vulnerabilities and ensuring the application's resilience against such attacks. Here's a breakdown of what DoS testing entails...

Testing for Anti-Automation Measures

- Captcha and Challenge-Response Tests: These tests are designed to differentiate between human users and automated bots. DoS testing verifies that these challenges are effective in preventing bots from launching automated attacks.
- Rate Limiting: This technique restricts the number of requests a user or IP address can send within a specific timeframe. Testing ensures that rate limiting is configured effectively to throttle suspicious activity without impacting legitimate users.

- Honey Pots and Honeypots: These are decoy systems that mimic real applications and attract attackers. Testing involves deploying honeypots to identify and analyze DoS attack attempts.

Account Lockout Mechanisms

- Login Attempt Thresholds: Implement thresholds for failed login attempts. Testing verifies that accounts are locked after exceeding a certain number of failed attempts within a timeframe, preventing brute-force attacks.
- Account Lockout Duration: The duration for which a locked account remains inaccessible is important. Testing ensures the lockout duration is long enough to deter attackers but not excessively long to inconvenience legitimate users.
- Account Lockout Notifications: Users should be notified when their account gets locked. Testing verifies that notification emails or messages are sent to inform users and potentially provide options to unlock their accounts securely.

Identifying DoS Vulnerabilities

- Resource Consumption Testing: Simulate DoS attacks by sending large volumes of requests to identify potential bottlenecks in the application or server infrastructure. This helps pinpoint areas that might be susceptible to overload during a real attack.
- Protocol and Logic Flaws: Certain vulnerabilities in application logic or protocols can be exploited for DoS attacks. Testing focuses on identifying such weaknesses and implementing appropriate security measures.
- Stress Testing: This involves simulating high volumes of legitimate traffic to assess the application's performance under load. While not strictly a DoS test, it helps identify potential weaknesses in scalability that could be exploited by attackers in a DoS scenario.

Business Logic Testing

Business logic testing is a crucial aspect of web application security testing that often gets overlooked. It delves beyond the technical implementation and focuses on the core functionalities of the application, how they interact, and potential vulnerabilities that could arise from flaws in the business logic itself.

What Business Logic Testing entails

- Misuse Cases: Think like an attacker and explore how the application's functionalities could be misused to achieve unauthorized actions. This might involve manipulating data, bypassing security checks, or exploiting loopholes in workflows. Example: In an e-commerce application, a tester might try manipulating product prices by tampering with data during checkout or exploiting a flaw in the order cancellation process to gain unauthorized refunds.
- Data Integrity Checks: Verify that the application maintains the accuracy and consistency of data throughout its various processes. This includes checking for scenarios where data can be tampered with or manipulated in unauthorized ways. Example: In a banking application, testers would ensure that account balances are always accurate and cannot be altered through unauthorized actions. They would also check for weaknesses that could allow attackers to inject fake transactions or manipulate account details.
- Segregation of Duties (SoD): This principle ensures that no single user has complete control over a critical business process. Testers verify that the application enforces SoD by preventing users from performing actions that could be used for malicious purposes. Example: In an accounting system, someone responsible for entering purchase orders should not have the ability to also approve payments for those orders. Business logic testing would ensure that the application enforces these separation rules.

Techniques for Business Logic Testing

- Threat modelling: This proactive approach involves identifying potential threats and vulnerabilities based on the application's functionalities and data flows.
- Manual Testing: Security professionals with an understanding of the application's business logic can manually explore different scenarios and identify potential misuse cases.
- Automated Testing: While not as comprehensive as manual testing, certain automated tools can be used to identify basic business logic flaws like missing authorization checks or data validation issues.

By incorporating Business Logic Testing into the overall security testing process, you significantly enhance the application's security posture by identifying and addressing vulnerabilities that could be exploited to compromise data, disrupt operations, or lead to financial losses.

Cryptography

Within the OWASP Web Application Security Testing Checklist, the Cryptography Assessment section focuses on evaluating how the application utilizes cryptographic techniques to safeguard data confidentiality and integrity. Here's a breakdown of what to look for:

Encryption Algorithms

- Strength: The application should employ robust and well-established encryption algorithms. Popular choices include AES (Advanced Encryption Standard) for symmetric encryption and RSA (Rivest-Shamir-Adleman) or ECC (Elliptic Curve Cryptography) for asymmetric encryption. Outdated or weak algorithms like DES (Data Encryption Standard) should be avoided.

- Data Classification: The chosen algorithm's strength should be appropriate for the data being protected. Highly sensitive data like financial information or personally identifiable information (PII) requires stronger encryption compared to less sensitive data.

Salting

- Presence: Verify that the application uses salting when storing passwords. Salting involves adding random data (the salt) to a password before hashing it. This prevents attackers from pre-computing rainbow tables, which can be used to crack common passwords easily.
- Salt Strength: The salt should be cryptographically secure random data with sufficient length (ideally at least 64 bits). A weak or predictable salt offers minimal protection.
- Unique Salts: Each user's password should be hashed with a unique salt. Reusing the same salt for multiple users makes them vulnerable if one password is compromised.

Key Management

- Secure Storage: Encryption keys should be securely stored, separate from the encrypted data. This could involve hardware security modules (HSMs) or dedicated key management systems.
- Key Rotation: Encryption keys should be rotated regularly to minimize the risk of compromise. Ideally, keys should be rotated at least annually or upon any suspected security breach.

Additional Considerations

- Hashing Algorithms: While not encryption itself, hashing algorithms play a crucial role in secure password storage. Verify that the application uses a strong, secure hashing algorithm like SHA-256 or bcrypt to hash passwords before storing them.

- Random Number Generation: Cryptographic functions often rely on randomness. Ensure the application uses a secure random number generator to avoid predictability in its cryptographic operations.

By thoroughly assessing these aspects, you can gain a good understanding of the application's cryptographic strength and identify any potential weaknesses that could expose sensitive data or compromise user accounts.

Risky Functionality

File Uploads and Payment Processing functionalities are particularly vulnerable if not properly secured. These functionalities introduce potential entry points for attackers to inject malicious code, steal sensitive data, or disrupt application functionality. Here's a breakdown of the security concerns and testing approaches for each...

File Uploads

- Vulnerability: Attackers can upload malicious files like scripts or executables that exploit vulnerabilities in the application or server. These files can then be executed on the server or by other users, compromising the system.

Testing Approach

- Allowed File Types: Verify that the application only accepts uploads of specific, allowed file types (e.g., images, documents). Restricting file types based on legitimate use cases helps mitigate risks.
- File Content Inspection: Scan uploaded files for malicious content using antivirus software or other detection tools. This helps identify hidden threats within files that might bypass basic file type checks.

- File Sanitization: Sanitize uploaded files to remove any potentially harmful code or scripts before storing them. This helps prevent exploitation even if malicious content manages to sneak past other checks.
- Secure Storage: Store uploaded files securely, ideally outside the web root directory. This reduces the risk of attackers accessing or tampering with uploaded files.

Payment Processing

- Vulnerability: Attackers can inject malicious code into payment forms or exploit vulnerabilities in the payment processing flow to steal credit card information or divert funds.

Testing Approach

- Secure Communication: Ensure all communication between the application, user, and payment gateway uses HTTPS to encrypt sensitive data like credit card details.
- Payment Tokenization: Consider using tokenization where sensitive financial data is replaced with a unique token during processing. This reduces the amount of sensitive data stored on the application server.
- Payment Gateway Security: Verify that the chosen payment gateway adheres to industry security standards like PCI DSS (Payment Card Industry Data Security Standard).
- Input Validation: Validate all user input related to payment information to prevent manipulation of amounts or account details.

By implementing these security measures and conducting thorough testing for file uploads and payment processing, you can significantly reduce the risk of financial losses and data breaches.

HTML5

HTML5 introduced several powerful features that enhance web application functionality but also require careful security consideration during testing. Here's a detailed look at some key areas of focus for HTML5 specific testing...

WebSockets

- Secure Communication: WebSockets enable real-time, two-way communication between a browser and a server. Ensure that the communication happens exclusively over secure connections (WSS- WebSockets Secure) using TLS/SSL encryption to protect sensitive data from eavesdropping or tampering.
- Authorization: WebSockets can be used to exchange sensitive data. Testing should verify that proper authorization mechanisms are in place to restrict access to authorized users and prevent unauthorized parties from joining WebSocket connections.
- Origin Validation: Implement origin validation to ensure that WebSockets can only be established with authorized origins (domains or subdomains). This helps prevent attackers from setting up malicious servers that impersonate the legitimate server.

Web Storage

- Storage Mechanisms: HTML5 offers various web storage mechanisms like Local Storage, Session Storage, and IndexedDB. Testers should assess how the application utilizes these mechanisms and ensure they are not used to store sensitive data in an insecure manner.
- Cross-Site Scripting (XSS): Data stored in Web Storage can be vulnerable to XSS attacks if not properly sanitized. Testing should focus on identifying and mitigating any potential XSS

vulnerabilities that could allow attackers to steal data stored in Web Storage.

- Content Security Policy (CSP): CSP can be used to restrict where web pages can load scripts from. Testing should ensure that CSP is configured appropriately to prevent malicious scripts from accessing data stored in Web Storage.

Cross-Origin Resource Sharing (CORS)

- CORS Configuration: CORS allows resources from one domain to be loaded by a web page from a different domain. Testers should verify that CORS is configured appropriately to restrict access to sensitive resources only from authorized origins. This helps prevent unauthorized websites from accessing or manipulating data on your application.
- SameSite Attribute: The SameSite attribute on cookies can be used to mitigate CSRF (Cross-Site Request Forgery) attacks. Testing should ensure that the SameSite attribute is configured appropriately to prevent cookies from being sent in cross-site requests.

By following this checklist, security professionals can systematically identify and address potential vulnerabilities in web applications, thereby enhancing their overall security posture and mitigating risks.

Conclusion - *The Future with OWASP*

The world of web application security is a relentless game of cat and mouse. Malicious actors are constantly innovating, devising new methods to exploit weaknesses in web applications and steal sensitive data. On the other side, security professionals must remain vigilant, proactively identifying, and patching vulnerabilities before they can be weaponized. In this ongoing battle, the OWASP (Open Web Application Security Project) project stands as a critical ally for developers, security specialists, and organizations of all sizes.

By following the OWASP Top 10, a dynamic list that constantly ranks the most critical web application security risks, you can significantly bolster the defenses of your web applications. This actionable list serves as a roadmap, prioritizing the areas that require the most immediate attention. Furthermore, incorporating the testing methodologies outlined earlier empowers you to conduct a comprehensive security assessment, pinpointing specific vulnerabilities that attackers might exploit. These best practices address fundamental weaknesses like injection attacks, insecure configurations, and broken access control mechanisms, forming a solid foundation for web application security.

However, security is not a one-time fix; it's an ongoing process that demands constant vigilance and adaptation. The threat landscape is ever-shifting, with new hacking techniques emerging all the time. To stay ahead of the curve, the OWASP project actively engages in several key initiatives:

Continuous Evolution of the Top 10: The OWASP Top 10 isn't a static list. It undergoes regular revisions to reflect the latest threats plaguing web applications. This ensures that security practices remain relevant and effective against the most contemporary hacking methods. By prioritizing the most critical risks, the OWASP Top 10 empowers developers to allocate resources efficiently and focus their efforts on areas that will yield the most significant security improvements.

Democratizing Security Knowledge: The OWASP website offers a treasure trove of free resources, including testing tools, cheat sheets, project guides, and educational materials. This empowers individuals and organizations to broaden their security knowledge and implement best practices, even with limited budgets. Free resources like these are instrumental in levelling the playing field and making web application security accessible to a wider range of actors. With a more knowledgeable and security-conscious developer base, the overall posture of the web application ecosystem improves.

Fostering a Global Community: One of OWASP's greatest strengths lies in its thriving global community of security professionals. This community functions as a vibrant hub for knowledge sharing, where experts from all over the world contribute their experience and expertise. This collaborative approach fuels the continuous development of new tools, methodologies, and best practices for web application security. By working together and sharing knowledge openly, the community can identify emerging threats faster, develop more effective defenses, and stay one step ahead of malicious actors.

Ultimately, by embracing the guidance offered by OWASP and actively engaging in security testing practices, you can build more secure web applications, protect sensitive data, and minimize the risk of falling victim to cyberattacks. Remember, security is a journey, not a destination. By staying informed, adapting your approach, and leveraging the resources offered by OWASP, you can ensure your web applications remain secure and resilient in the face of evolving threats. Furthermore, by contributing to and engaging with the OWASP community, you can play a part in creating a safer digital world for everyone. As the web application security landscape continues to evolve, OWASP will undoubtedly remain a vital resource in this ongoing battle to protect the integrity of the web.

***

About the Author

Rajesh Dangi is a technologist, author, mentor and key note speaker with over three decades of accomplished experience in Information Technology (IT) domain, A diversified background in in the areas of IT infrastructure, Cloud computing, Emerging technologies such as AI/ML, Application & Data Engineering, Open source systems and is a certified ISO27K lead auditor and Project management professional.

On personal front he has authored several blogs, articles and published technology books, Sci-Fi, poetry in Marathi, Hindi and English, besides he is a social activist, foodie, photographer and loves long drives and farming. He is based out of Bangalore, India.

Twitter: @rajesh_dangi

Email: rajesh_dangi@yahoo.com

LinkedIn : https://www.linkedin.com/in/rajeshdangi/